ST. MARY'S COLLEGE OF MARYLAND
ST. MARY'S CITY, MARYLAND

CZECHOSLOVAK
STORIES

CZECHOSLOVAK STORIES

TRANSLATED FROM THE ORIGINAL AND
EDITED WITH AN INTRODUCTION BY

ŠÁRKA B. HRBKOVA

*Professor of Slavonic Languages and Literatures
at the University of Nebraska (1908-1919)*

Short Story Index Reprint Series

BOOKS FOR LIBRARIES PRESS
FREEPORT, NEW YORK

First Published 1920
Reprinted 1970

STANDARD BOOK NUMBER:
8369-3556-X

LIBRARY OF CONGRESS CATALOG CARD NUMBER:
71-122723

PRINTED IN THE UNITED STATES OF AMERICA

TO
THE LITTLE MOTHER

Who, loving her children's America, kept ever
blooming, in her new home, a garden of the
sweet flowers of Czech and Slovak literature.

CONTENTS

	PAGE
Introduction	1
Svatopluk Čech	51
Foltýn's Drum	55
Jan Neruda	71
The Vampire	75
Beneš	81
At the Sign of the Three Lilies	86
He Was a Rascal	90
František Xavier Svoboda	101
Every Fifth Man	105
Joseph Svatopluk Machar	119
Theories of Heroism	123
Božena Víková-Kunětická	133
Spiritless	135
Božena Němcová	145
"Bewitched Bára"	151
Alois Jirásek	221
The Philosophers	225
Ignát Herrman	231
What Is Omitted from the Cook-book of Madame Magdálena Dobromila Rettigová	233
Jan Klecanda	239
For the Land of His Fathers	241

CONTENTS

	PAGE
Caroline Světlá	277
Barbara	279
Appendix A	319
Appendix B	321
Appendix C	329

CZECHOSLOVAK STORIES

CZECHOSLOVAK STORIES

INTRODUCTION

THE CZECHOSLOVAKS AND THEIR LITERATURE

THE literature of the nation of Czechoslovaks is as ancient as its history. For a period of over a thousand years, the literature of no nation is more closely entwined with its history than is that of the people composing the new Czechoslovak Republic.

When the first despatches began to appear in English and American newspapers relative to the exploits of the Czechoslovak troops in Russia and Siberia, the average reader asked: "Who are these new people? What new nation is this that has sprung into prominence as a friend to the Allies?"

It was necessary to enlighten many even of more than usual intelligence and to inform the general public that it was no new, strange race of whose brave deeds they were reading but only the old and oft-tested nation of the Czech inhabitants of Bohemia in northwestern Austria and of the Slovaks of northern Hungary, the name "Czechoslovak" being formed by combining the two words "Czech" and "Slovak" by means of the conjunctive "o." The Czechoslovaks are, therefore, the direct descendants of John Huss, Komenský (Comenius), Kollár, Palácký, Havliček and a thousand other staunch upholders of the truth and right, torchbearers of Europe.

The Czechs had chafed under Austrian misrule since the fateful day when, in a period of Bohemia's weakness, the Hapsburgs gained control of the little country which, geographically, forms the very heart of Europe and in many another way has been the organ which sent the blood pulsating freely and vigorously through the body of the Old World. The Slovaks have suffered even greater persecutions with no chance of redress from the Magyar (Hungarian) population which forms the southeastern portion of what was once the Dual Empire.

It was no wonder, therefore, that the Czechs and Slovaks, enduring for ages the persecutions of German and Magyar, and in past periods knowing too well that they were but tools for Hapsburg ambition which forgot the promised reward of independence when its own selfish objects were attained, lined themselves to a man on the side of justice and democracy when the clarion call went round the world. There was no written summons, not even an uttered determination but when the man power of Austria-Hungary was mobilized, the Czechs and Slovaks, forced into the Hapsburg armies, looked significantly at each other. That look meant

INTRODUCTION

"We shall meet in Serbia, Russia, Italy, France"—according to the front against which they were sent.

The story of the Czechs and Slovaks, subjects of Francis Joseph, fighting on the side of Serbia and Italy to whose armies they had made their way in some inexplicable manner, drifted through now and then to the American public. But, most marvelous was the feat of those thousands of Slav soldiers, who, at their first opportunity, deserted to Russia—there to reorganize themselves into strong fighting units on the side where lay their sympathies.

Then came the downfall of the Russian Revolution and the collapse of the whole national morale. The Treaty of Brest-Litovsk freed hundreds of thousands of German and Magyar war-prisoners in Russia. The Red Army was formed, threatening the vast supplies on the Trans-Siberian railway.

Separated, by thousands of miles, from their homes, the Czechoslovaks, a mere handful in the midst of the millions of German and Magyar freed war-prisoners of Siberia who led the vast armies of the Bolsheviki, present a picture of unexampled dauntlessness, of splendid courage with only the hope of the attainment of their country's freedom to spur them on amidst their bleak and bloody five years' isolation. It is, indeed, a theme for an epic. It remains to be seen whether that epic shall be written in the Anglo-Saxon tongue or in the language of those whose noble efforts achieved the recognition and the independence of Czechoslovakia.

A nation producing the quality of men who never forgot what they were striving for even though the struggle was centuries old arouses the interest of the thinking public. Whence came the strength of purpose of these representatives of so small a country? The Czechoslovak Republic comprises, with the combined areas of the former kingdom of Bohemia, margraviate of Moravia, duchy of Silesia and province of Slovakia but 50,000 square miles of territory and some 12,000,000 of people. Where then is its power? Surely not in the extent of its realm or the number of its inhabitants.

"Not by might, but by the spirit shall ye conquer" is the motto that has been sung by every Czechoslovak poet and writer. Its philosophers have added "Only of free and enlightened individuals, can we make a free and enlightened nation."

It can truly be said that the writers among the Czechs and Slovaks have been the teachers and saviours of their nation.

In no land has literature as such played a greater part in educating and developing national instinct and ideals. In countries untrammelled by the rigors of a stiff Austrian censorship of every spoken word, it is possible to train patriots in schools, auditoriums, churches. The confiscation of Czech newspapers for even a remote criticism of the Hapsburg government was a regular thing long before the exigencies of war made such a proceeding somewhat excusable.

INTRODUCTION

It was then through belles-lettres that the training for freedom had to come. And the writers of the nation were ready for they had been prepared for the task by the spiritual inheritance from their inspired predecessors. And so it came about that in their effort to express the soul of the nation they told in every form of literature of the struggles to maintain lofty aspirations and spiritual ideals.

The literature of the Czechs and Slovaks groups itself naturally into three main periods—just as does the history of their land.

1. The Early period beginning with the inception of writing in the Czech language to the time of John Huss (1415) with its climax in the fourteenth century.

2. The Middle period reaching its height in the sixteenth century and closing with the downfall of the nation after the Battle of White Mountain, in the middle of the seventeenth century. (Only a few desultory efforts mark the early part of the eighteenth century.)

3. The Modern period opening with the renaissance of the Czech literary language at the end of the eighteenth century and including the marvelous development of the present century.

Only a few names of each period can be included in this brief survey.

EARLY PERIOD

The oldest writings in the old Slavonic which was brought to Bohemia by the missionaries, Cyril and

Methodius, date back to the ninth century, when the Czechs and Moravians accepted Christianity.

The Chronicles of Kristian telling of the martyrdom of Saint Ludmila and Václav belong to the tenth century, the historical writings of Kosmas, dean of the Prague chapter (1045–1125) following soon after as did also "The Chronicles of Dalimil."

The authenticity of the beautiful poems composing the famous Kralodvorský Rukopis (Queen's Court Manuscript) has been questioned by the Czechs themselves and cannot, therefore, be included in a list on which no doubts can be cast.

The oldest authentic single piece of literature is the stately church song "Hospodine Pomiluj ny" (Lord, Have Mercy) belonging to the eleventh century. Some years later came the epic "Alexandrine" telling of the Macedonian hero and a whole series of the legends of the saints. Magister Záviš, composed many liturgies as well as worldly poems. He was later in life a professor in the University of Prague which was established in 1348, being the first institution of higher education in Central Europe, antedating the first German university by half a century. The Czech language for the purposes of literature developed several centuries in advance of German which did not become a fixed literary language until the sixteenth century when Luther completed his translation of the Bible.

Smil Flaška, a nephew of Archbishop Arnošt of Pardubice, composed in 1394–5 poetry both didactic

INTRODUCTION

and allegorical, under the titles "Nová Rada" (New Counsel) and "Rada Otce Synovi" (Advice of a Father to His Son). He presents the ideal of a Czech Christian gentleman of his period.

In fact in the period just preceding John Huss, practically all writing was religious or chiefly instructive though satire and a bit of worldliness crept even into the writings of certain famous Prague priests notably the Augustinian Konrad Valdhauser and Jan Milič of Kroměříž who inspired Tomáš of Štítný (1331-1401), the earliest really great prose writer of the Czechs. The latter was among the first students of the University of Prague, founded by Karel IV. (the same Charles I. who ruled the Holy Roman Empire). He wrote in the spirit of Milič, his first work being "Řeči Besední" (Social Talks) in which he philosophizes and gives information about God, the creation and fall of man, of man's struggles to shun sin and attain wisdom. He wrote many other volumes on the same order, in a pleasing and careful manner which remain as examples of pure and correct Czech of his time.

MIDDLE PERIOD

The second period of Czech literature was ushered in by the greatest figure in Bohemia's eventful history, Jan Hus (John Huss). His birth date is variously given —1364 to 1369. Hus was at once a preacher, writer, teacher, reformer, patriot, prophet, martyr. To him truth was the most sacred thing on earth. Not one jot would he recede from a position once taken for the cause of that one white changeless essential—Truth. Every sermon he preached as minister of the Bethlehem Church, every address he uttered as rector of the University of Prague had the essence of the shining spiritual, moral and intellectual progress for which he lived and for which he was burned at the stake on the 6th of July, 1415, at Constance. While numberless volumes by Hus were destroyed in the course of a systematic search undertaken with the purpose of exterminating them, his wonderful Letters, written from Constance, his "Postilla Nedělní" (Sunday Postilla), "Dcerka," (The Daughter) showing the right path to salvation, "Zrcadlo Člověka" (Mirror of Man), "Svatokupectví" (Simony) have been preserved as a heritage to the world. As the leader of the Bohemian Reformation which took place over a hundred years before the far easier one of Luther's time, as a patriot and writer upholding his nation's rights and ideals, he stands preeminent.

The simplification of the Czech written language is also to the credit of this ceaselessly active man who devised the present system of accents for vowels and consonants to take the place of endless and confusing combinations of letters. The nation owes him a further debt for the introduction into the church service of many beautiful hymns of his own composition and others which he translated.

A successor of Jan Hus in the fight for a pure and

unsullied faith was Petr Chelčický whose works, the Postilla or Sunday readings, "Siť Víry" (The Net of Faith) and O šelmě (Of the Beast of Prey) largely influenced Count Leo Tolstoi in forming his non-resistance theory. The Net of Faith especially expounded a simple religion free of the hypocrisy and evil of the nobility and of the cities, living on the labor of the producing class. He advocates at that early date (1390–1460) the separation of church from state. Jan Rokycana, archbishop of Prague, on his return from exile after George of Poděbrad gained control of the capital, though not a prolific writer, was an inspiring speaker and left as a monument the church of the Bohemian and Moravian Brethren which carried out in its tenets the essentials which he advocated for true Christians in his writings and speeches. Strangely enough, in later years, he turned against the Brethren whose first firmest supporters were his own pupils.

The contention of all these writers and leaders of thought in Bohemia in the Middle Ages was to the effect that the only true source of the pure law of God was the Bible. It is not to be wondered at that the translation of the Bible, completed near the close of the fourteenth century, was distributed in innumerable hand-written copies, some of which were most beautifully ornamented as, for instance, the Dražďanská Bible (Dresden) made in 1400–1410, and the Olomouc copy in two parts (1417). The first printed Bible in the Czech language was from a new and improved translation and appeared in Prague in 1488 though the New Testament had already been printed in 1475.

The Bohemian and Moravian Brethren maintained printing houses in Mladý Boleslav and Litomyšl from which were issued catechisms, bibles, song-books, sermons and other religious works urging the simple Christian faith and spirit of brotherly love as a sure means of securing the Kingdom of God on this earth. Throughout there was close observation of the humanistic teachings of Chelčicky whose popularity served to make every one eager to read with the result that the literary language became more stabilized and literary activity was enthusiastically encouraged.

For a century and a half writers of varying degrees of power produced a great quantity of books largely religious, didactic, polemical, philosophic, historical, political, and scientific but there was relatively little of poetry or of purely creative literature in this period.

One name stands pre-eminent in connection with the disastrous crisis of the Battle of White Mountain. John Amos Komenský (Comenius) 1592–1670—last bishop of the Bohemian and Moravian Brethren and first apostle of scientific education—the father of modern educational methods—belongs among the shining lights of all nations and not alone to the land that gave him birth. Being the last bishop of the Bohemian and Moravian Brethren, he fell a victim to the orgies of hatred practised by the conquerors of the Bohemian Revolt when on November 8, 1620, the adherents of

INTRODUCTION 11

complete independence from Hapsburg jurisdiction were overwhelmingly vanquished. On the battle-field of Bílá Hora (White Mountain), Bohemia lost its independence and the devastation wrought by passing and repassing armies in the dread Thirty Years War left the country prostrate for two full centuries. There were no means, in those days, of summoning a sympathetic and open-handed world as was done in 1914 to the aid of a suffering Belgium. Bohemia in 1620 was, like Belgium, the victim of wars in the forming of which its chief crime(?) was its geographical location. But in the seventeenth century, means of communication, of transportation for bounteous supplies to succour the needy were not developed as they were three centuries later when organized relief for a wronged nation was the united response of all but the offenders against international law.

It was in the early days of that period that John Amos Komenský, encouraging his nation to the last, preached a doctrine of universal peace, of settlement of international differences by arbitration instead of by wars, of a peace and joy securable only through the practice of true and genuine Christianity. He urged education for all classes and training of the heart as well as of the mind as a means of overcoming future ills, misunderstandings and national catastrophes. But he was not merely a preacher, he was an enactor of his own doctrines whose efficacy has been proved by three centuries of practice.

Komenský's most noteworthy contributions to the literature and culture of his people and of all nations include an elaborate Czech-Latin and Latin-Czech dictionary; a versified version of the Psalms in the Czech language; "Labyrint Svĕta a Ráj Srdce" (The Labyrinth of the World and the Paradise of the Heart), published in 1631, the predecessor of Bunyan's "Pilgrim's Progress" giving in exquisite form the struggles of man to attain perfect happiness and harmony of soul, the work being more distinctly pure literature in a technical sense than any of his other writings. It was translated into English by Count Francis Lutzow in 1905. The "Magna Didactica" or Great Didactic was written originally in the Czech language and Englished by M. W. Keating. In this he lays out a system of education forming the basis of all modern progressive plans to-day. The "Janua Linguarum Reserata" or Gate of Tongues Unlocked simplified the process of learning Latin and other tongues. It was written in exile in Poland after Komenský like thousands of other non-Catholics had been expelled from his native land by the edict of 1627 directed against the Brethren and was translated into twelve European languages and also certain eastern tongues as the Persian, Arabian, Turkish, etc. The *Orbis Sensualium Pictus* or the World in Pictures, the first illustrated school text-book for children ever published, prepared the way for the magnificent pictorial features in educational texts of the present day.

INTRODUCTION

The "Informatorium Školy Matěrské" gave invaluable aid in the rearing of young children in the so-called "Mother School."

Komenský might have been numbered among the educational reformers of our own country for Cotton Mather writes of his visit to the famous educator whom he invited to become president of the then newly organized Harvard College in the American Colonies. For some reason Komenský did not accept though his wanderings, after his exile from Bohemia were many and varied. His life's pilgrimage ended in 1670 at Amsterdam where he had lived during the last fourteen years of so busy and useful a life of service to education that he has been entitled, without challenge, the "teacher of nations."

After Komenský, there were no great writers in the Czech language until the close of the eighteenth century. It must be remembered that every effort was made to suppress not only the language of the Czechs but to prevent the publication of any work in that tongue. The Jesuit, Antonín Koniáš (d. 1760) boasted that he alone had destroyed some 60,000 Czech books. He published a "Key to Heretical Errors of Doctrine" which comprised the names of objectionable religious books to be consigned to the flames on sight.

Those who owned Czech Bibles or other books in the language of their fathers, were punished for having them in their possession. Hence they took the greatest precautions in secreting such volumes as, despite the terror, they were able to treasure and hand down from father to son.

MODERN PERIOD

RENAISSANCE

The modern period of Czech and Slovak literature divides itself automatically with the history of the nation into two natural groupings:

1. The literature of the national renaissance, from the close of the eighteenth century to 1848. This in turn, is subdivided into the period of enlightenment (1780–1815) and the period of romanticism (1815–1848).

2. The literature of the revivified nation, from 1848 to the present day.

The retrogression, in a national sense, brought about by Maria Theresa and Joseph II. in the wholesale introduction of the German language in place of the vernacular was counteracted, in a sense, by the truly great social, economic and religious reforms which were brought about by the enactments: in 1774 of a law organizing public schools; in 1775 of the annulment of serfdom and of feudalism; in 1781 by the passing of the Toleration Patent permitting religious freedom.

Almost immediately scientific and literary organizations and writers sprang up in Bohemia and among the Slovaks. The efforts of Joseph II. at centralization in the Hapsburg Empire by means of the exclusive use of the German without recognition of the language of the

INTRODUCTION 15

numerous linguistic groups composing the realm, led to political opposition. The voice of the newly awakened Czech nation refused to be hushed and the result was the re-establishment at the ancient Czech University of Prague of a chair of the Czech language and literature, by royal decree, on the 28th of October, 1791. František Martin Pelcl was the first professor in charge of the work, laying the foundation for national self-consciousness among the brightest intellects of the land. The significance of the Hapsburg concession of 1791 is evident to-day in the enlightened and intelligent national coherence of the Czechoslovaks every one of whose responsible leaders in the movement for absolute independence were university trained men.

Joseph Dobrovský, a member of the Jesuit order, prepared valuable critical studies of the Czech, Slovak and other Slavonic languages dealing with their value as literary vehicles without a shadow of chauvinistic tendency. Indeed, though he rendered inestimable aid by his philological studies, he failed to foresee the rich literary future for the languages into whose intricacies he delved as a scientist.

The popularization of history, philosophy, of all sciences and arts and knowledge occupied such men as Václav Matěj Kramerius, founder of numerous newspapers and other periodical publications; Antonín J. Puchmajer, writer of many lovely lyrics expressed in purest Czech; Antonín Bernolák, noted Slovak and advocate of a separatist policy who chose as the vehicle for his valuable discussions the West-Slovak dialect; Václav Thám, author of many popular dramas and other plays instrumental in awakening the national spirit.

The romantic period of the renaissance affected not only Czech and Slovak literature, but it left its imprint on all the arts—on philosophy, religion, the sciences, and political, social and moral life. The protest of rich imagination, of unfettered freedom in feeling and expression against the cold reasoning and polished conventionality of the eighteenth century found its outlet among the Czechs and Slovaks in an enthusiastic exaltation of their nation and language—two concepts never separated in the mind of the true patriot of that land.

Gradually the idea of nationality broadened to include all that was Slavic. The poetic and prose enthusiasts wove beautiful and inspiring tapestries with the background of Panslavism but few, indeed, among them carried the idea through, even in thought, to a practical platform of mutuality in culture, science, industries and politics. The romantic period exemplified and enriched the resources of the native tongue for lyrical purposes while supplying grammarians and philologists with material for scientific national expansion. Political progress was prepared for by the advancement made in the popularization of historical works. Invaluable publications like the Journal of the Museum of the Kingdom of Bohemia, the "Matice

Česká" (Mother of Čechia), "Česká Včela" (Czech Bee), "Krok," "Květy České" (Czech Blossoms) and "Czechoslav" gathered and presented to the public the really worthy writings of that and preceding periods.

Among the chief writers in this significant era certain men are representative.

Prof. Jan Nejedlý was the successor of Pelcl in the chair of the Czech language and literature at the University of Prague. Nejedlý's chief service does not rest so much in his worthy translations into Czech of the *Iliad* and of modern writings such as Young's "Night-Thoughts," but rather in his assembling in his quarterly publication "The Czech Herald" all the older authors and of practically all the younger exponents of romanticism.

Joseph Jungmann, was the composer of the first Czech sonnets in which he sang of love, patriotism, public events, of the chivalrous deeds of the early Czechs, of the ideals of Slav unity. A whole school of poets clustered about Jungmann and followed his leadership. He translated into richly flowing Czech many works of Oliver Goldsmith, Alexander Pope, Gray, Goethe, Schiller, Herder, Chateaubriand and Milton's "Paradise Lost." A monumental "Dictionary of the Czech Language and its Relationships to the other Slavic Tongues" is the master work of Jungmann's life. It was the labor of fully thirty-five years and ordinarily would have occupied the time of entire faculties of universities. It was published in October, 1834.

Jan Evangel Purkyně although best known in science as a pioneer physiologist especially for his studies of the human eye, and as the founder of the laboratory method which he formulated as professor of physiology at Vratislav and later established in the University of Prague in whose medical faculty he served as the most prominent European authority for fully twenty years, was nevertheless active in a literary way, producing many essays, some poems and valuable translations of Tasso's "Jerusalem" and Schiller's lyrics.

Jan Kollár, the idol of Slovak literature, after a thorough education completed by careful theological studies devoted himself to the cause of his people in the Protestant church in Budapest which he was called to serve and where he remained for thirty years despite frequent attacks from both Germans and Magyars. His chief bequest to the Czechoslovak people is his collection of poems entitled "Slávy Dcera" (The Daughter of Sláva). The word "Sláva" admits of two interpretations—"Glory" and "Slavia," the allegorical representation of the entire Slavic group just as "Columbia" stands for America. In the poems, Kollár addressed his inspired sonnets to Slavia in whom are at once blended the conceptions of the daughter of the mythical goddess of the Slavs and of his sweetheart, Mina. In this collection, printed a hundred years ago, Kollár, in numerous songs argues for the union of all the Slav groups and predicts that vast progressive changes and wondrous achievements will be realized by each of the Slavic peoples a century hence. He foretells the recognition and use of the Czech and other Slavic tongues at mighty courts and in palaces where the Slav speech shall no longer be a Cinderella as in times past. The distinguished feats of his countrymen on many battlefields in the Great World War and the attainment of the independence of the Czechoslovaks as a result, would seem to show Kollár was a true prophet as well as a great poet.

František Palacký stands foremost among the historians of Bohemia, his work "Dějiny Národu Českého" (History of the Czech Nation) being accepted as absolutely authoritative and quoted as such by scholars of all nations. Palacký's previous writings show his wide range of culture and knowledge. He founded and edited the Journal of the Museum of the Kingdom of Bohemia, as well as several other publications significant of the spirit of the awakening in Bohemia. His scholarly work "The Beginnings of Czech Poetry Especially of Prosody" mark his early Slavonic inclination. Many philosophic and critical essays deal mainly with æsthetic development. His political writings, particularly his discussions of "Centralization and National Equality in Austria" and "The Idea of the Austrian State," have been widely quoted. It was Palacký who in 1848 asserted with the vision of a seer "We existed before Austria and we shall exist after there will be no Austria."

The Slovak writer, Pavel Josef Šafařik, is second only to Kollár in the affection of his countrymen. He began his literary career as a poet at nineteen when his collection "The Carpathian Muse with a Slavonic Lyre" was published. Later, through the assistance of Palacký, he removed from Slovakia to Prague devoting himself indefatigably to a work of rare quality—"Slovanské Starožitnosti" (Slavonic Antiquities) in which he showed the ancient origin of the Slavs, and proved by an enormous number of authoritative documents and other evidence their early civilization and culture and their linguistic, topographic and historical relationship to the members of the Indo-European group of languages.

František Ladislav Čelakovský, intended for the priesthood like so many Czech literary men, early gave up the plan of his parents and devoted himself to Slavistic and poetic studies. He had gathered great numbers of folk songs, poems and sayings which last were eventually included in a collection entitled "Mudrosloví Národu Slovanského v Příslovích" (The Philosophy of the Slavic Nation in its Proverbs). His first original work was his collection of epics "Ohlasy Písní Ruských" (Echoes of Russian Songs) which he later augmented by his lyrical "Ohlasy Písní Českých" (Echoes of Czech Songs). Palacký regarded this work as of equal worth with Kollár's "Slávy Dcera."

Karel Jaromír Erben collected a vast quantity of folk songs and tales which he wove into delicate and beautiful poems. His first collection "Kytice" (The Bouquet) by its beauty and harmonious arrangement gave earnest of the treasures to come. This collection was translated into practically every European language. His "Folk and National Songs of the Czechs," were followed by "Sto Prostonárodních Pohádek a Pověstí" (One Hundred Folk Tales and Legends) and by the "Vybrané Báje a Pověsti Národní Jiných Větví Slovanských" (Selected National Myths and Legends of Other Slavic Branches).

Karel Hynek Mácha, the gifted Czech successor to the peculiar spirit and genius of Byron, is a pioneer in the romantic movement in his country. Though he died in his twenty-sixth year, he had given incontrovertible evidence of his leadership in this field in his lyrics, ballads, and hymns and in his longer production "Máj" (May) which aroused at once a chorus of approval from the Byronic rhapsodists and of stinging censure from the critics, who because they did not admire his philosophy refused to evaluate properly the beauty and perfection of Mácha's poetic art which did not win appreciation until long after his death. Of his short stories, the best is "Márinka," a daring and realistic genre of the proletariat.

To this period also belong the early dramatists, Václav Kliment Klicpera (1792–1859) author of a series of historical plays and comedies some of which are still performed and Josef Kajetan Tyl who early left his university studies to organize a traveling theatrical company producing only Czech plays. Tyl wrote and produced over thirty exceedingly popular plays many of which like certain ones of his novels were summarily criticized by Havlíček for an extreme sentimentalism in their patriotic teachings.

In one of his comedies, Tyl inserted a poem entitled "Where is My Home?" which from the initial presentation won instant favor and was adopted as the national hymn of the Czechoslovaks.

WHERE IS MY HOME? (KDE DOMOV MŮJ?)

Where is my home?
Where is my home?
Waters murmur o'er its fair leas,
Hills are green with rustling fir-trees,
Flow'rets bright with Spring's perfumes,
A Paradise on earth it blooms,
That's the land of loveliest beauty
Čechia, my motherland!
Čechia, my motherland!

Where is my home?
Where is my home?
In God's beloved land are found
True gentle souls in bodies sound,
A happy peace which clear minds sow,
A strength defying warring foe.
Such are Čechia's noble children
'Mongst the Čechs, my motherland!
'Mongst the Čechs, my motherland!

To the present day, Tyl's "Strakonický Dudák" (The Bagpipe Player of Strakonits) a beautiful fairy drama, his "Paličova Dcera" (The Incendiary's Daughter) and "České Amazonky" (The Czech Amazons) are still favorites.

Prokop Chocholoušek, journalist and correspondent, led an adventurous life whose rich and varied experi-

INTRODUCTION

ences are frequently utilized in his stories. In his collection of short stories "Jih" (The South), he first opened to Prague readers the story lore of the Slavs of the Balkans whose struggles for liberty he had witnessed.

František Jaromír Rubeš, at first wrote poems of a patriotic nature the best being his "Já jsem Čech" (I am a Czech) but his chief contribution to his nation's literature is in his distinctive and deliciously humorous stories of the provincials of city and country life. His best stories are "Pan Amanuensis" (The Amanuensis), "Pan Trouba" (Mr. Fool) and "Ostří Hoši" (Clever Chaps).

Ludevítú Štúr, a Slovak poet and publicist, did much through his essays, poems and stories to defend his people against the violent Magyarization practised sedulously by the Hungarians.

Jos. M. Hurban, a Slovak realistic writer, rendered invaluable service to his nation not only by his own well-conceived and excellently presented stories of his people but by the founding of a Slovak review which became the repository of the most worthy literary treasures of the language.

FROM 1848 TO THE PRESENT DAY

In the second part of the modern period of the literature of the Czechs and Slovaks or that which is expressive of the nation after 1848, an impressive host of writers appears. In no other equal space of time has a

NOTE.—Ten of the important authors of this period are treated in detail in sketches preceding each story, hence they are merely mentioned in this summary.

nation produced so many literary works of unquestioned merit. The revival of letters is complete. Standards are established but constantly advanced by the demand not only of critics but of the authors themselves and their very readers. Critics demand sincerity and depth instead of mawkish sentimentalism, forcefulness and energy instead of the old time "beautiful resignation" or Oblomovesque inertia.

Karel Havlíček Borovský undeniably stands foremost as intolerant of the patriotism of the lips which never reaches the reality of deeds. Just as bitter is he in his judgment of authors drifting aimlessly in their work. He was in his early youth an intense Russophile thinking to attain Slav unity by the submergence of the other Slavic dialects. But after a year spent in Russia he returned fully cured of the idea. He brought back, however, a keen admiration for N. Gogol whose stories he translated and a study of whose style made Havlíček the best epigramist of his times. His "Pictures from Russia" show his keenness of observation and clear conception of true democracy. Undertaking the editorship of the Pražské Noviny (Prague News) and "Česká Včela" (Czech Bee), he made them the leading literary and critical publications, the latter journal being universally known as "the conscience of the Czech Nation." He was active politically being a representative to the Vienna parliament in 1848–1849. In his Národní Noviny (National News) which he began to publish April 5, 1848, he was the voice of the

INTRODUCTION 25

nation which responded as only a politically awakened and intelligent national constituency can respond. Undaunted he attacked the great hulking body of the Austrian government, reeking with sores and ugly with its age-old unfulfilled promises to the nations which composed it. He demanded a constitution with full political freedom but he was as firm in his denunciation of a radical revolution. He urged separation of church and state, insisted on full educational opportunities for all clasess—in rural districts as well as in cities. He rejected Russian paternalism and sympathized with the Poles and Southern Slavs.

His style is simple, clear, direct, forceful. He never missed making his point. By the clarity and precision of his short incisive sentences, he made it possible for the people to follow him in teachings of the most progressive and advanced sort. But the Austrian government could not, of course, brook the untrammelled presence of a man of Havlíček's imposing and inspiring personality. His paper was confiscated again and again. Journals which he founded elsewhere did not long elude the censor. Prosecution and persecution followed ultimately. At the end of 1851 Havlíček was deported to Brixen in the Tyrol where he contracted tuberculosis. It was here he wrote his unequalled satires "Tyrolské Elegie" (Tyrol Elegies) and "Král Lávra" (King Lávra). Practically a dying man he was permitted to return to his native land where he found that in the meantime his wife had died. His own death soon followed on the twenty-ninth of August, 1856.

In the first years of this period Václav B. Nebeský wrote poetry of a strain whose innate beauty alone makes it valuable, to be sure, but whose chief interest rests in the fact that it became a sort of standard of modern tendencies for all the younger poets as Jan Neruda himself acknowledges. He encouraged a whole host of young writers as for instance Němcová to earnest literary effort.

Karel Sabina wrote short stories and novels in which sociological questions are brought up as in his "Synové Světla" (Sons of Light) which was later published under the title "Na Poušti" (On the Desert) and also in his story of political prisoners "Oživené Hroby" (Enlivened Graves). He wrote clever librettos for a number of popular operas among them Smetana's "Prodaná Nevěsta" (The Bartered Bride) in which the Czech prima donna, Emma Destinnova, has sung the leading part in American performances.

Jan Neruda is usually classed with Vitězslav Hálek because they were the leaders of the enthusiastic literary men of the period—in the main, youths of twenty or thereabout who devoted every ounce of energy to their muse and their nation. They made the new literature reflect their own ideals of social equality, religious liberty, better advantages and fairer treatment of the laboring classes, emancipation of women, free self-expression.

INTRODUCTION

Vitězslav Hálek wrote many ballads and lyrics, the collections entitled "Večerní Písně" (Evening Songs) and "V Přírodě" (With Nature) having been models for many writers and as much quoted as Longfellow. An allegorical representation of the struggles of the nation in the seventeenth century is his long poem "Dědicové Bílé Hory" (Heirs of White Mountain). An idyll of the Slovák mountains is his "Děvče z Tater" (The Girl from the Carpathians). His short stories present some intensely interesting character studies as well as plots depending on incident for their interest.

NOT ANY OF THESE HAVE AS YET BEEN TRANSLATED INTO ENGLISH

Adolf Heyduk stands nearest of kin to the Hálek-Neruda school in his beautiful lyrics "Ciganské Melodie" (Gypsy Melodies), "Cymbál a Husle" (The Cymbal and Violin) "Ptačí Motivy" (Bird Motives). He ever sings of the happy life, of young love, family joys, loyalty to the homeland, the beauties of nature especially of the Slovák and Šumava mountains. He is wholesome and cheerful without ever overstepping into rhapsodical inanities.

Realistic writers arose who would not follow the old romantic trend and who depicted more and more of the individual home and national problems with a devotion which was bound to wean the public away from the conventional novel of pure sentiment and unreal figures. Chief among them was Božena Němcová whose nearest rival in the field of the realistic novel is another woman—Karolina Světlá.

Gustav Pfleger Moravský's best work is his novel of the laboring classes "Z Malého Světa" (From a Small World) which is significant as the first psychological study in literature of the struggle of labor with capital and the attempt to create a new social order.

Václav Vl. Tomek, called "the Historian of Prague," is the successor as an authority in the source method as well as of literary style of his distinguished predecessor, Frant. Palácký. Antonín Gindely organized the Czech archives and drew on them as well as on the documentary sources in France, Germany, Belgium, Holland and Spain for the material for his histories of the period of John Amos Komenský and the Bohemian and Moravian Brethren. Joseph Emler published hitherto unknown "Original Sources of Czech History." August Sedláček's chief contribution is a monumental work on "The Castles, Palaces and Citadels of the Kingdom of Bohemia," written in interesting literary manner as was also his "Historic Legends and Traditions of the Czech People in Bohemia, Moravia and Silesia." Dr. Arne Novák, Dr. J. V. Novák and J. Vlčeh have written extensive and valuable histories of Czech and Slovák literature.

MODERN DRAMATIC LITERATURE

Joseph Jiří Kolar (1812–1896) is called the "Father of Modern Dramatic Literature" among the Czechs.

INTRODUCTION

He was the first Czech to translate Shakespeare's plays and to stage them. Numerous translators of the English bard have appeared at frequent intervals in Bohemia but Kolar's poetical adaptations of Hamlet, Macbeth, The Taming of the Shrew and The Merchant of Venice were the accepted stage versions for many decades though his translations of the other Shakespearean dramas failed of as favorable a reception. Goethe's Faust, Goetz von Berlichingen and Egmont and Schiller's trilogy on the life of Wallenstein and his "Robbers" also were translated by Kolar. It was later that the playwright who was likewise a successful actor and director wrote, using the plan of the Shakespearean dramas, a series of original plays—namely tragedies and historical dramas which have survived the test of time. The best are "Královna Barbora" (Queen Barbara), "Monika" (Monica), "Pražský Žid" (The Jew of Prague), "Žižkova Smrt" (The Death of Žižka), "Mistr Jeroným" (Magister Jerome).

František A. Šubert, the real organizer of the Czech drama, has paid glowing tributes to Klicpera. He has written many thoroughly excellent dramas with historical or semi-historical backgrounds, among them "Probuzenci" (The Awakened Ones), "Petr Vok Rožmberk," "Jan Výrava" a five act drama of the period of the closing days of feudalism, translated into English by Šárka B. Hrbkova. Problems of live social and economical interest which are unsolved to-day are considered in his "Praktikus" (The Practical

Man); "Žně" (The Harvest), and "Drama Čtyř Chudých Stěn" (A Drama of Four Poor Walls) translated into English by Beatrice Měkota.

Ladislav Stroupežnický has written many frequently produced realistic comedies as "Pan Měsíček," "Paní Mincmistrová" (The Mintmaster's Wife), "Naši Furianti" (Our Braggarts).

M. A. Šimáček sketches some interesting factory types in his studies of the sugar-beet industry which he also uses in his plays.

Gabriella Preissova brought the Slovenes of Carinthia into Czech and Slovák literature and is the author of the delightful "Obrázky ze Slovácka" (Pictures from Slovakia) as well as of very successful Slovák plays "Gazdina Roba" and "Její Pastorkyňa" (Her Stepdaughter).

Joseph Štolba has written ten plays chiefly comedies which continue to win audiences as well as readers.

Jaroslav Kvapil is at once a lyric poet uniting gentle, deep emotion with form that is distinctly pleasing. His best collections are "Padající Hvězdy" (Falling Stars) and "Růžový Keř" (The Rose Bush). He has written successful dramas as: "Oblaka" (The Clouds) translated into Russian and German, and into English by Charles Recht; "Bludička" (The Will o' the Wisp) English translated by Šárka B. Hrbkova; the fairy plays "Princezna Pampeliška" (Princess Dandelion) and "Sirotek" (The Orphan) suggest somewhat the influence of Maeterlinck. He has translated into Czech

INTRODUCTION 31

several of Ibsen's plays in which his wonderfully talented wife, the celebrated actress Hana Kvapilova, played the leading rôle.

Alois and Vilém Mrštík, two brothers, collaborated in the collection of stories called "Bavlnkovy Ženy" (The Cotton Women) and in the play "Maryša" though the former wrote independently many lovely stories of the Slovaks in the Carpathian region and the latter many naturalistic tales.

Karel Pippich has written one valuable drama, "Slavomam" (The Greed for Glory), and some comedies.

COSMOPOLITANISM OF CZECH LITERATURE

The cosmopolitanism of modern Czech literature is apparent in many prodigiously industrious writers not only active in their translations from foreign literatures but remarkable for their output of thoroughly good original matter—poems, novels, dramas and short stories. These writers through travel and wide reading in the literatures of other lands have imbibed the spirit of those countries which they present in literary masterpieces. The Czechs and Slováks no longer are content to be provincial, the local traditions do not suffice. The themes which other nations admire they examine and discuss through the means afforded by their own gifted literary interpreters.

Joseph V. Sládek was one of the first Czech literary men to visit America. As a youth of twenty-four who had just finished his philosophical and scientific studies in Prague, he came to the United States, remaining here for two impressionable years, the spirit of which is clearly discernible in many of his best poems particularly his lyrics and sonnets of which several volumes were published. Sládek's stay in America had another result and that was the translation of Longfellow's "The Song of Hiawatha" as well as of many single poems by individual American poets. He also translated Bret Harte's "California Stories" and Aldrich's "Tragedy of Stillwater" both of which proved very popular among Czech readers. Sládek made translations of "Frithiof" by the Swedish poet Tegner, the romance "Pepita Ximenes" from the Spanish of J. Valera, "Conrad Wallenrod" from the Polish of A. Mickiewicz, the "Hebrew Melodies" of Byron, ballads of Robert Burns and poems of Samuel Taylor Coleridge.

Julius Zeyer (1841–1901) though excelling as a lyric and epic poet has to his credit many volumes of successful novels, short stories, and dramas the subjects of most of which are culled from other than home fields. In his travels which included frequent trips to Russia, Vienna, Germany, Paris, Switzerland, Sweden, Italy, Greece, Constantinople, Spain, the Tyrol, Styria, Carniola, Croatia, the Crimea, he gathered impressions and motives which were later woven into his poems and stories. Thus in his lyric "Igor" and his novels "Darija" and "Ondřej Černyšev" (Andrew Černyšev) there is a clear echo of months spent in Russia; in his

INTRODUCTION

"Blanka" (Blanche) an intimation of troubadour days in the Provence; in the love of "Olgerd Gejstor" for the Czech Queen Anne, there is the distinctive Lithuanian background; the romance "Gabriel de Espinos" and the tragedy of "Dona Sancha" evince the Spanish influence; in "Ghismonda" and more clearly in his semi-autobiographical novel "Jan Marya Plojhar" appears the Italian influence; the novel "Dům u Tonoucí Hvězdy" (The House of the Waning Star) is the consequence of his sojourn in France; in the "Chronicles of Saint Brandon" and "The Return of Ossian" his Irish studies are evident. Just as faithful is he in giving the Czech and Slovák atmosphere as for instance in "Raduz a Mahulena," a fairy tale of the Slovák region, "Neklan" and "Vyšehrad" of the pagan Czech period, "Duhový Pták" (The Rainbow Bird) a novel of modern Bohemia.

Jaroslav Vrchlický (Emil Frida) the most prolific and versatile writer of the nation, deserves to be named likewise its greatest cosmopolite. Thoroughly travelled and with deep knowledge of all ancient and modern civilizations to which he gives expression in his works, he fully deserves the title. His original poems alone fill sixty-four generous volumes, his prose tales, novels and dramas are represented in some twenty or more volumes, not to speak of his valuable critical and literary essays of which there are at least a dozen volumes. To these must be added an immense number of unparalleled translations from the literatures of practically all cultured nations, ancient and modern, and then only can a fair conception be had of the marvellous labors and the unequalled significance to Czech literature of this indefatigable individual, who has created more real literature than is contributed ordinarily by an entire generation of writers.

The immensity of the task of a review of this author's activity is apparent. Only the mention of a few of his achievements is possible. His "Zlomky Epopeje" (Fragments of an Epopee) represents the attempt of the author to trace through ballads, romances, legends and myths the development of man from the beginning to the present time, the whole permeated with his own peculiar philosophy of history which insists on the triumph of man over matter and of self-sacrificing love over all other human manifestations. The "Bar Kochba" is a magnificent epic of the desperate and heartbreaking struggle of the Jews against Rome. His "Legenda Sv. Prokopa" (Legend of St. Procopius) employs Czech historical material exclusively. Of five volumes of sonnets, the most popular has been the collection "Sonnets of a Recluse." Many of his twenty-four books of lyrics have gone into several editions. Among them are "Rok na Jihu" (A Year in the South); "Motýli Všech Barev" (Butterflies of all Tints) "Na Domácí Půdě" (On Home Soil), "Pavučiny" (Cobwebs) and "Kytky Aster" (Bouquets of Asters). Of the volumes devoted to the philosophic contemplation of the basic facts of life, love and death, the best are his "Písně Poutníka" (Songs of a Pilgrim), "Vittoria Colonna" "Pantheon," "Bodláčí z Parnassu" (Thistles from Parnassus) and "Já Nechal Svět Jít Kolem" (I Let the World Pass By).

Vrchlický's best dramas depict characters and events of ancient times with Czech, Greek, Roman, Spanish, Italian, English or pure mythological backgrounds. The list includes twenty-eight plays—chiefly dramas or tragedies practically every one of which has been produced. A number of these have been translated into English.

Of four collections of short stories the most successful has been the "Barevné Střepy" (Colored Fragments). "Studies of Czech Poets" is a most valuable and elaborate work as are also his critical essays on Modern French poets dealing mainly with the school of Victor Hugo of whom he was a great admirer.

Through his truly amazing diligence in translation, Vrchlický opened to the Czech reading public new worlds of literature, his aim being to interest especially the younger generation in the rich treasures of all nations. His superior genius made it possible to give the precious lore of other times and other lands a thoroughly artistic rendering in his mother tongue in which he has been acknowledged master by all the critics of his day.

One stands aghast at the mere linguistic knowledge necessary to comprehend the delicate intricacies of the poetic lore of the French, Italian, Spanish, Portuguese,

English, German, Polish, Magyar, Scandinavian and even Chinese without even speaking of his rare ability in presenting in beautiful Czech equivalent the spirit and content of the authors translated. He showed most conclusively the rich possibilities of his native tongue as a vehicle for the noblest of thoughts and technically for the transference of the most difficult rhymes and meters in modern European literature.

Victor Hugo, Leconte de Lisle, Corneille, Molière, Beaudelaire, Dumas, France, Maupassant, Balzac, Rostand, Petrarch, Dante, Ariosto, Tasso, Michelangelo, Parini, Leopardi, Carducci, Gracosa, Anno Vivanti, Cannizzaro, Camoens, Echegaray, Verdaguer, Mickiewicz, Arany, Petofi, Hafiz, Shi King, Byron, Swinburne, Browning, Shelley, Tennyson, Whitman, Poe, Schiller, Goethe, Hamerling, Ibsen, Andersen— the masterpieces of all these were worthily made known to his countrymen through the untiring energy of Vrchlický.

While Vrchlický is now more fully appreciated in his own land, he has not escaped criticism which at times has been bitterly harsh, especially in the '70's when it was thought he should choose subjects oftener from the history of the Czech nation. Then, too, as the originator of such vast stores of literature, it is not a matter of wonder that the critics charged him with technical and formal errors, with banalities and improvisations. Yet withal Vrchlický stands as a master among masters, who was slave to no school, who felt the deepest, most

INTRODUCTION

fundamental manifestations of life and expressed them clearly, forcefully, beautifully without the dimming mask of rhetorical flourish.

The Vrchlický schools of writers imitate him in his technical verse construction and echo his thoughts of deep-seated world sorrow, wide sympathy for his fellow-men, longing for the moral and social regeneration of mankind, the hope of ultimate freedom from the existent destructive religious scepticism.

Among later poetic translators from the English is Antonín Klášterský who first acquainted his countrymen with the poems of John Hay, Bryant, Lowell, Lee Hamilton, Elizabeth Barrett Browning, Oscar Wilde, Joaquin Miller, Sidney Lanier, Stedman.

Eliška Krásnohorská whose real name is Eliška Pechová became a leader of her sex from the time, in 1870, when she entered literature in her twenty-third year. In 1875 she founded and has continued to serve as editor of the "Ženské Listy" (Woman's Journal). She organized the "Minerva" society which in 1890 founded an advanced school for women students. As the guiding spirit of the Women's Industrial Society organized by Caroline Světlá she has, as has Božena Kunětická in a degree, rendered unmeasured service to the practical cause of women. These activities have lent their spirit to her literary productions, especially her poems which are full of the urge to practical, substantial patriotism, of appeal to aid the cause of the Balkan Slavs or other isolated Slavic groups or to recognize the just aspirations of her own sex. She never rhapsodizes without effect and her feelings, sounding deep and ringing true, are ever purposeful. The best collections are "Na Živé Struně" (On a Living String), "Vlny v Proudu" (Waves in the Current), "K Slovanskému Jihu" (To the Slavonic South) "Letorosty" (Sprigs) and "Povídky" (Stories).

She wrote unusually clever librettos for Smetana's operas "Hubička" (The Kiss) and "Tajemství" (The Secret), for Zděnek Fibich's "Blaník" (Mount Blanik) and for Bendl's "Lejla" and "Karel Škréta." Her translations were chiefly from Alex. Puškin (Boris Godunov) and Selected Poems, Hamerling (King of Zion) Lord Byron (Childe Harold's Pilgrimage), Adam Mickiewicz (Pan Tadeusz).

She has produced great numbers of stories for children and sketches and novels appearing in women's magazines though by no means limited to that sex for readers.

BOOKS OF SCIENCE

Valuable books of travel and discovery have been written by numerous Czech explorers and "globetrotters." Among them are: Joseph Kořenský who wrote "A Trip Around the World"; Jiří Guth, "A Causerie of Travel" digesting in many volumes the philosophy of the nations visited; Dr. Emil Holub, who explored South Africa and wrote several volumes on his numerous trips; Pavel Durdik who with wonderful interest discussed his "Five Years in Sumatra."

INTRODUCTION 39

Dr. Jan Gebauer wrote many invaluable philological works and as an authority was ranged on the side opposing the authenticity of the famous Queen's Court Manuscripts.

Dr. Fr. Drtina professor of pedagogy and Dr. Fr. Krejčí professor of psychology of the faculty of the University of Prague are like Prof. Masaryk, of the positivist school and have written valuable philosophical discussions on the subjects of their life study as has also Prof. Fr. Čáda, likewise a philosopher.

HISTORICAL NOVELISTS

Undoubtedly the foremost figure in this group is Alois Jirásek who has devoted himself exclusively to the rich material offered by the aspirations and struggles of his native land. Třebízský and Winter have been only a little less active in this field.

Václav Beneš Třebízský, completed the theological course in Prague, was ordained in 1875 and served as chaplain from that time until his death. Most of his works are shorter than novels, of which the best are his "Anežka Přemyslovna" a story of the era of Václav I.; "Královna Dagmar" (Queen Dagmar) "Trnová Koruna" (The Crown of Thorns) of the period of the Thirty Years' War and "Bludné Duše" (Lost Souls) descriptive of the religious strife during the reign of Joseph II. Many collections of his stirring short stories, some ninety in all, based on the events in Czech history appear under the titles "Pod Doškovými

Střechami" (Under Thatched Roofs) "V Záři Kalicha" (In the Glow of the Chalice) and "Z Různých Dob" (From Various Epochs). His engaging and attractive style, the genuineness of his sympathy with his subjects unite in making his works popular for readers of all ages.

Zikmund Winter as professor of history had ample opportunity to collect interesting and valuable material but his decision to use it in literature came in later years when he vividly reconstructed early Prague life from the documents and archives at his disposal, weaving vigorous characters into the ancient atmosphere. His more noteworthy collections are "Rakovnické Obrázky" (Pictures from Rakovnik) "Pražské Obrázky" (Prague Pictures), "Miniatury" (Miniatures) and "Mister Kampanus" (Magister Kampanus) a pretentious story of student life of the period succeeding the Battle of White Mountain which he regards from a partisan viewpoint.

SHORT STORIES

A group of writers arose after Neruda who carried to extremes his declaration that brief genre pictures representing small segments of contemporary life with devotion to every-day detail and with a lively sense for character outline could form an eventual channel for realistic story telling. The result was an almost slavish adherence to insignificant trivialities and a parceling out, among the story writers, of specialized fields of "proficience" forgetting form and real substance for

INTRODUCTION 41

fidelity to detail. Then, too, a class of writers arose who consistently surrendered themselves to "temperament" refusing to recognize any law of utilitarianism, or technical form. The middle-of-the-road writers followed the spirit of Neruda's teaching and renounced the policy of the pure æstheticians.

In the new period were the following writers: František Herites, character delineator in his "Z mého Herbáře" (From My Herbarium) and "Tajemství Strýce Josefa" (Uncle Joseph's Secret).

Jakub Arbes wrote stories of mysterious or misanthropic, fantastic characters, but endowed them with his own world views. His best stories are "Ďábel na Skřipci" (The Devil on the Rack), "Ethiopská Lilie" (The Ethiopian Lily), "Newtonův Mozek" (Newton's Brain) "Svatý Xavier" (Saint Xavier).

Sofie Podlipská, a sister of the famous Karolina Světlá, was likewise active though her work was mainly in juvenile and feministic literature.

Alois Vojtěch Šmilovský, another realist, has painted some small town, moralist, and old world types which he has blended into rather attractive romantic settings. His "Nebesa" (Heavens) has been translated. Other very good short stories are in the extensive collections published between 1871 and 1896.

Jan Herben often in humorous vein yet with a world of sympathy delineates Slovák peasant life. Karel V. Rais, poet and popular short story writer, depicts the conditions of life among the mountaineers and villagers in simple but appealing tales. Joseph Holeček an advocate of unity with South Slavonic culture and an opponent of all contact with Germanism, is author of "Hercegovinian Songs," "Serbian National Epics," "Montenegro." Teréza Nováková represents the cause of her sex in many public movements and in her books details the sorrowful fate of women who seek moral self-determination in the midst of a social system that simply does not understand. Karel Klostermann is the novelist and story teller of the glass-blowers, woodmen, poachers, and lumbermen of the border regions. Bohumil Havlasa presents fantastic adventures, exotic experiences. Jan Havlasa, son of Jan Klecanda, after several years spent in the United States wrote some interesting "California Stories." Jos. K. Šlejhar uncovers in the so-called "best families" a world of petty tyrannies, cruelties and bestialities practised by those wearing the cloak of respectability. Jiří Karásek writes of decadence and occultism. Růžena Svobodová exposes in her masterful and well-nigh scientific manner the frailties and gnawing sores of each social stratum and turns the light on the pitiable condition of so many women who, ignorant of their own purpose in life, live in hopeless dreams until, spiritually famished, they perish in their own illusions, amid the joyless drab of life. Martin Kukučin, the leading Slovák realist, in addition to portraying his own people as he knew them has presented intimate views of the Croatian and Serbian peasantry. Svetozár Hurban

Vajanský is a Slovák writer, ten volumes of whose poems, short stories and novels have been published in Sv. Martin.

Among poets of high order who expressed the most advanced spiritual interests in the present day stands a trio headed by Joseph S. Machar with Otakar Březina the chief symbolist and lyric visionary and Antonín Sova ever seeking psychological bases and portraying some crisis of the soul. P. Selver, an English poet, and O. Kotouč, an American have translated many typical lyrics by this trio.

Viktor Dyk has written numerous poems in a sceptical, satirical vein and is also the author of some incisive short stories and dramas. Petr Bezruč whose real name is Vladimir Vašek "first bard of Beskyd," is unqualifiedly the true singer of Silesia whose bitter fate of denationalization at the hands of the Germans and Poles he lamented in lyrical lines inspiring his brother Czechs over the border to render what aid they could before submergence was complete.

No review of Czech and Slovák literature could be counted complete if it omitted Thomas G. Masaryk. The man who to-day is president of the newly created Czechoslovak Republic has been a leader of thought in his native land for nearly two decades. Born March 7, 1850, in Hodonin, Moravia, of a Slovák father and Moravian "Hanák" mother, he had all the experiences incident to laboring families of insufficient means, before he finished the gymnasium in Brno and his philosophical studies at Vienna. He traveled in Germany and Russia and upon his return was named a member of the faculty of the University of Prague in 1882, attaining the rank of a full professorship in 1896. In 1902 and again in 1907 he visited the United States of America from which country he chose his bride, Miss Alice Garrigue of Boston. He took an active part in politics as early as 1891 from which time he was a representative, at intervals, of his country at the Vienna parliament. When Austria-Hungary declared war in July 1914, Prof. Masaryk raised his voice against the ultimatum delivered to Serbia. Because it was everywhere known that Prof. Masaryk had already exposed forgeries on the part of Austrian government agents in previous attempts to foment trouble with the Balkan Slav states, and because Masaryk was the acknowledged leader of his people, he was immediately a man marked for imprisonment and even execution by the Hapsburg government. However, the story of Prof. Masaryk's escape to Switzerland and then his journey to the courts and leading ministries of England, France, Russia, and the United States to present the case for independence of the Czechoslovaks and the record of how the tens of thousands of his soldier countrymen conducted a campaign of separatism from Austria-Hungary though far distant from their homeland, as was their leader also, is now a matter of history. It suffices that all maps of Europe will now bear the name of the free and independent government of

INTRODUCTION

Czechoslovakia—and that the united action of a thoroughly capable leader and a trained and intelligent nation achieved the consummation of the national aspirations of centuries.

Prof. Masaryk's contributions to the literature of his country began in 1876 with an article on "Theory and Practice," his first philosophical essay being "Plato Jako Vlastenec" (Plato as a Patriot) published the following year.

A division took place in the university faculty relative to the methods of philosophy—whether it should be critical or encyclopedic. The first party contended that the work of the Czech scientists should be severely judged according to the strictest foreign standards. The others urged the systematization of all knowledge and its popularization. Thomas Masaryk solved the question for himself and followers by establishing a scientific-critical journal, the Athenæum (1883) and by planning the collecting of all known knowledge to be embraced in the monumental "Ottův Náučný Slovník" (Otto Encyclopedia). This encyclopedia up to 1910 had published over 150,000 titles on 28,912 pages and had employed 1100 literary co-workers.

Three branches of practical philosophy interested Masaryk chiefly: sociology, the philosophy of history and the philosophy of religion. To the period of study of these subjects belong his briefer psychological discussions: "Hypnotism" (1880), "Blaise Pascal" (1883), "A Theory of History According to the Principles of

T. H. Buckle" (1884), "Slavonic Studies" (1889), "The Fundamentals of Concrete Logic" (1885).

When the struggle to revive and renew Czech cultural life became the most critical, Masaryk presented a series of analytic studies of Bohemia's literary and political revival. These are widely published and read in America also and included his "Karel Havlíček" (1896), "Jan Hus—Naše Obrození a Naše Reformace" (Jan Hus—Our Renaissance and Our Reformation) (1896), "Česká Otázka" (The Czech Question) (1895), "Naše Nynější Krise" (Our Present Crisis) (1895). His "Otázka Socialní" (The Socialist Problem) analyzes and appraises Marx and his principles. "V Boji o Naboženství" (The Struggle of Religion), "Mnohoženství a Jednoženství" (Polygamy and Monogamy) (1902), "V Boji Proti Alkoholismu" (The Fight Against Alcoholism) (1908), "Česká Filosofie" (Czech Philosophy) (1912), all contain the ripe judgment of a man who had thoroughly digested the problems discussed.

In each article and book Masaryk's remarkable personality stands forth in his determination, first, to wholly emancipate the Czechs from the German philosophy, accomplishing this by supplanting Kant with Hume, Herbart with English psychology, not merely by interpretation but by a critical reorganization into which his own ethical and religious convictions entered; second, by bringing philosophy down from a plane of mere theory to become the first aid in all sciences, arts, religion and every-day life so that the

INTRODUCTION 47

actions of the nation and of the individuals composing it would intelligently, systematically and purposefully lead to a definite goal. In his "Czech Philosophy" Masaryk wrote in 1912 "Pure Humanity, signifying the only genuine brotherhood is the ideal of the Czech renaissance and represents the national program as handed down from early generations of Czech leaders. The Czech ideal of humanity—the Czech ideal of Brotherhood must become the leading thought of all mankind."—Thus, through great teachers a nation of earnest students has been trained to effectively carry out a great idea in the practical school of world politics and statesmanship.

Reading maketh a full man.

CZECHOSLOVAK STORIES

49-50

SVATOPLUK ČECH

(Born February 21, 1846, in Ostředek near Benešov.
Died February 23, 1908.)

SVATOPLUK ČECH was the son of a government official, and thus spent his youth in various parts of his native land, attending schools in Postupice, Liten, Vrány, Litoměřice and Prague, securing his degree in the Piaristic Gymnasium in 1865. Later, he studied law, though as a Gymnasium student he had already entered the field of literary effort, using the pseudonym "S. Rak." Eventually he became editor successively of several of the leading Czech literary journals. His best works appeared in the "Květy" (Blossoms), a magazine which he and his brother, Vladimír, established in 1878.

Čech traveled extensively in Moravia, Poland, the Ukraine, around the Black Sea, Constantinople, in the Caucasus, Asia Minor, Denmark, France and England. Each of these journeys bore literary fruit.

While Čech is unquestionably the greatest epic poet of the Czechoslovaks and by some critics is ranked as the leading modern epic poet of Europe, some of his shorter prose writings are also notable as examples of enduring literature.

Čech's title to superlative distinction in the field of poetry is earned through the following works which discuss broad humanitarian, religious and political questions with democratic solutions in each case. "Adamité" (The Adamites) is an epic of the Reformation describing the rise and fall of this peculiar religious sect. "Bouře" (Tempests) and "Sny" (Dreams) are in the Byronic manner. "Čerkes" is a picture of the life of a Czech immigrant in the Caucasus. "Evropa" (Europe) studies the forces disintegrating ancient Europe. "Ve Stínu Lípu" (In the Shade of the Linden Tree) depicts with rich touches of delicate humor such types as the simple peasant, the upstart tailor-politician, the portly miller, the one-legged soldier and others, each relating experiences of his youth, a veritable Czech "Canterbury Tales." In "Václav z Michalovic" he presents a sorrowful epic of the gray days after the Battle of White Mountain. "Slavie" is a truly Utopian picture of Panslavism. "Dagmar" unites the threads binding Czech with Danish history. "Lešetinský Kovář" (The Blacksmith of Lešetin), a distinctively nationalistic poem, dramatically portrays the struggles of the Czechs against the insidious methods of Germanization. This poem was suppressed in 1883 and not released until 1899, being again prohibited after August, 1914, by the Austrian government. Portions of this vividly genuine picture have been translated into English by Jeffrey D. Hrbek.

SVATOPLUK ČECH

"Petrklíče" and "Hanuman" are collections of lovely fairy tales and plays in Čech's most delightful verse. "Modlitby k Neznámému" (Prayers to the Unknown) is a series of meditations in pantheistic vein on the mysteries of the universe. "Zpěvník Jana Buriana" (The Song Book of Jan Burian) solves monarchistic tendency with the one true answer — democracy. "Písně Otroka" (Songs of a Slave), of which some fifty editions have been published, not only in Bohemia, but in the United States as well, represent, through the symbolism of oriental slavery, the modern bondmen who are in mental, moral, political and industrial subjection.

Of his larger prose works, the novels "Kandidát Nesmrtelnosti" (A Candidate for Immortality) and "Ikaros" are best known, but humor and satire, together with genuine story-telling ability, hold the reader far more tensely in his delicious "Výlet Páně Broučkův do Měsíce" (Mr. Brouček's Trip to the Moon) and in his ten or twelve collections of short stories, arabesques and travel sketches. The story "Foltýn's Drum" is selected from Čech's "Fourth Book of Stories and Arabesques."

FOLTÝN'S DRUM

BY SVATOPLUK CECH

Old Foltýn hung on his shoulder his huge drum, venerable relic of glorious patriarchal ages, and went out in front of the castle. It seemed as if indulgent time had spared the drummer for the sake of the drum. The tall, bony figure of Foltýn—standing in erect perpendicularity in soldier fashion, wrapped in a sort of uhlan cape, with a face folded in numberless furrows, in which, however, traces of fresh color and bright blue eyes preserved a youthful appearance, with a bristly gray beard and gray stubble on his double chin, a broad scar on his forehead, and a dignified uniformity in every motion—was the living remnant of the former splendor of the nobility.

Old Foltýn was the gate-keeper at the castle, an honor which was an inheritance in the Foltýn family. As in the Middle Ages, vassal families devoted themselves exclusively to the service of their ruler, so the Foltýn family for many generations had limited its ambitions to the rank of gate-keepers, stewards, granary-masters, herdsmen and game-wardens in the service of the noble proprietors of the castle. Indeed one member of the family had become a footman for one of the former masters and thereby the boast and proud memory of his numerous kinsmen.

Well then, old Foltýn stepped forth with his drum before the castle, to all appearances as if he wished to drum forth the mayor and the councilmen to some exceedingly important official duty, but in truth, alas, to noisefully assemble an army of old women to their work on the noble domain.

He slightly inclined his head and swung the sticks over the ancient drum. But what was that? After several promising beginnings he suddenly concluded his performance by a faint tap. I am convinced that many an old woman, hearing that single indistinct sound, dropped her spoon in amazement and pricked up her ears. When that mysterious sound was followed by no other she doubtless threw a shawl over her gray braids and running to the cottage across the way, met its occupant and read on her lips the same question her own were forming: "What happened to old Foltýn that he finished his afternoon artistic performance with such an unheard of turn?"

It happened thus: If you had stood in Foltýn's place at the stated moment and if you had had his falcon eyes you would have descried beyond the wood at the turn of the wagon-road some sort of dark object which with magic swiftness approached the village. Later you would have distinguished a pair of horses and a carriage of a type never before seen in those regions.

When the gate-keeper had arrived at this result of his observation, he recovered suddenly from the absolute petrifaction into which he had been bewitched by the appearance of the object and raced as fast as his legs would allow back to the castle.

Beruška, the steward's assistant, was just bidding a painful farewell to a beautiful cut of the roast over which the fork of his chief was ominously hovering when Foltýn with his drum burst into the room without even rapping. He presented a remarkable appearance. He was as white as chalk, his eyes were staring blankly, on his forehead were beads of sweat, while he moved his lips dumbly and waved his drumstick in the air. With astonishment all turned from the table toward him and were terrified in advance at the news whose dreadful import was clearly manifested in the features of the old man.

"The nob—nobility!" he stuttered after a while.

"Wh—what?" burst forth the steward, dropping his fork on the plate.

"The nobility—beyond the wood—" answered Foltýn with terrible earnestness.

The steward leaped from his place at the table, seized his Sunday coat and began, in his confusion, to draw it on over his striped dressing-gown. His wife, for some unaccountable reason, began to collect the silver from the table. Miss Melanie swished as she fled across the room. Beruška alone stood unmoved, looking with quiet satisfaction at his chief, whom

Nemesis had suddenly overtaken at his customary culling of the choicest pieces of the roast.

In order to interpret these events I must explain that our castle, possibly for its distance and lack of conveniences, was very little in favor with its proprietors. From the period of the now deceased old master, who sojourned here a short time before his death, it had not beheld a single member of the noble family within its weatherbeaten walls. The rooms on the first floor, reserved for the nobility, were filled with superfluous luxury. The spiders, their only occupants, let themselves down on fine threads from the glitteringly colored ceilings to the soft carpets and wove their delicate webs around the ornamentally carved arms of chairs, upholstered in velvet. The officials and servants in the castle knew their masters only by hearsay. They painted them as they could, with ideal colors, to be sure. From letters, from various rumors carried from one manor to the next, from imagination, they put together pictures of all these personages who, from a distance, like gods, with invisible hands reached out and controlled their destinies. In clear outlines there appeared the images of barons, baronesses, the young baronets and sisters, the maids, nurses, the wrinkled, bewigged proctor, the English governess with a sharp nose, the fat footman, and the peculiarities of each were known to them to the minutest detail. But to behold these constant objects of their dreams and discussions, these ideals of theirs, face to face, was for them a prospect at once blinding and terrifying.

In the castle, feverish excitement reigned. From the upper rooms echoed the creaking of folding-doors, the noise of furniture being pushed hither and thither, the whisking of brooms and brushes. The steward's wife ran about the courtyard from the chicken house to the stables without a definite purpose. The steward hunted up various keys and day-books and charged the blame for all the disorder on the head of Beruška, who, suspecting nothing, was just then in the office, rubbing perfumed oil on his blond hair. Old Foltýn stood erect in the driveway with his drum swung from his shoulder, every muscle in his face twitching violently as he extended his hand with the drumstick in the direction of the approaching carriage as if, like Joshua of old, he execrated it, commanding it to tarry in the village until all was in readiness. Through his old brain there flashed visions of splendidly ornamented portals, maids of honor, schoolboys, an address of welcome, flowers on the pathway. . . . But the carriage did not pause. With the speed of the wind it approached the castle. One could already see on the road from the village the handsome bays with flowing, bright manes and the liveried coachman glittering on the box. A blue-gray cloud of dust arose above the carriage and enveloped a group of gaping children along the wayside. Hardly had Foltýn stepped aside a little and doffed his shaggy cap, hardly had the soft white silhouette of Melanie disappeared in the ground-floor window, when the eminent visitors rattled into the driveway.

In the carriage sat a gentleman and a lady. He was of middle age, wore elegant black clothes and had a smooth, oval, white face with deep shadows around the eyes. He appeared fatigued and sleepy, and yawned at times. The lady was young, a fresh-looking brunette with a fiery, active glance. She was dressed in light colors and with a sort of humorous, coquettish smile she gazed all around.

When they entered the driveway, where practically all the occupants of the castle welcomed them with respectful curtsies, the dark gentleman fixed his weary, drowsy eyes on old Foltýn who stood in the foreground with loosely hanging moustaches, with endless devotion in his honest blue eyes, and with an expression of contrite grief in his wrinkled face, his patriarchal drum at his hip.

The baron looked intently for a while at this interesting relic of the inheritance from his ancestors, then the muscles of the languid face twitched and his lordship relieved his mood by loud, candid laughter. The bystanders looked for a moment with surprise from the baron to the gate-keeper and back again. Then they regarded it as wise to express their loyalty by blind imitation of his unmistakable example and they all laughed the best they knew how. The steward and his wife laughed somewhat constrainedly,

FOLTÝN'S DRUM 61

the light-minded Beruška and the coachman with the lackey, most heartily. Even the baroness smiled slightly in the most bewitching manner.

Old Foltýn at that moment presented a picture which it is not easy to describe. He looked around several times, paled and reddened by turns, patted down his cape and gray beard in embarrassment and his gaze finally slid to the fatal drum. It seemed to him that he comprehended it all. He was crushed.

After a few condescending words to the others the nobility betook themselves to their quarters, leaving for the time being on the occupants of the lower floors the impression that they were the most handsome and the happiest couple in all the world.

After a while we behold both in the general reception-room. The master rocks carelessly in the easy-chair and sketches a likeness of old Foltýn on the covers of some book. The baroness, holding in her hand a naked antique statuette, looks about the room searchingly.

"Advise me, Henry. Where shall I place it?"

"You should have left it where it was."

"Not at all! We are inseparable. I would have been lonesome for these tender, oval, marble features."

"But if you haul her around this way over the world she won't last whole very long."

"Never fear! I'll guard her like the apple of my eye. You saw that I held the box containing her on my lap throughout the journey."

"You might better get a pug-dog, my dear!"

The baroness flashed an angry glance at her husband. Her lips opened to make response to his offensive levity, but she thought better of it. She held the statuette carefully and swished disdainfully past the baron in the direction of a rounded niche in the wall. She was just about to deposit her charming burden when suddenly, as if stung by a serpent, she recoiled and extended a finger towards her husband. The dust of many years accumulated in the niche had left its gray trace.

"Look!" she cried.

"Look!" he repeated, pointing towards the ceiling. From the bouquet of fantastic flowers there hung a long, floating cobweb on which an ugly spider was distinctly swinging.

"You wouldn't listen to my warnings. Well, here you have an introduction to that heavenly rural idyll of which you raved."

The baroness drew down her lips in disgust at the spider and in displeasure at her husband's remark. Violently she rang the bell on the table. The fat footman in his purple livery appeared.

"Tell them down below to send some girl here to wipe down the dust and cobwebs," the lovely mistress said to him with frowning brow. She sat down opposite her husband, who was smiling rather maliciously, and gazed with vexation at her beloved statuette.

A considerable time passed, but no maid appeared.

The baroness showed even greater displeasure in her countenance, while the baron smiled more maliciously than ever.

The footman's message caused great terror below on account of the dust and the cobwebs and no less embarrassment on account of the request for a maid. After long deliberation and discussion they seized upon Foltýn's Marianka as a drowning man grasps at a straw. After many admonitions from old Foltýn who hoped through his daughter to make up for the unfortunate drum, they drew out the resisting girl from the gate-keeper's lodge. The steward's wife with her own hands forced on Marianka her own yellow silk kerchief with long fringe which she folded across her bosom, placed an immense sweeping-brush in her hands, and thus arrayed the footman led his trembling victim into the master's apartments.

The baroness had just stamped her foot angrily and approached the door when it softly opened and Marianka, pale as the wall, with downcast eye, appeared in it. The unkind greeting was checked on the baroness' lips. The charm of the simple maid surprised her. Slender she was and supple as a reed, her features gentle and childishly rounded, the rich brown hair contrasting wonderfully with her fresh white skin, and her whole appearance breathing the enchantment of earliest springtime.

"Here, dear child!" she said to her, agreeably, pointing to the floating cobweb.

The girl bowed awkwardly, and for an instant under her light lashes there was a flash of dark blue as she stepped timidly forward. The brush did not reach the cobweb. She had to step up on her tiptoes. Her entire face flushed with a beautiful red glow, her dark-blue eye lifted itself towards the ceiling, her delicate white throat was in full outline, and below it there appeared among the fringes of the yellow shawl a string of imitation corals on the snowwhite folds of her blouse. Add to this the dainty foot of a princess and acknowledge—it was an alluring picture.

When all that was objectionable had been removed, the baroness tapped Marianka graciously on the shoulder and asked, "What is your name?"

"Marie Foltýnova," whispered the girl.

"Foltýn? Foltýn? What is your father?"

"The gate-keeper, your Grace!"

"Doubtless the man with the drum," suggested the baron, and a light smile passed over his face.

"Go into the next room and wait for me," said the baroness to the girl. When she had departed, the baroness turned to her husband with these words: "A charming maiden. What do you think of her?"

"Well, it's a matter of taste."

"I say—charming! Unusually beautiful figure, a most winsome face and withal—such modesty!"

"The statuette is threatened with a rival."

"Jokes aside, what do you say to my training her

to be a lady's maid? To taking her into service? What do you say to it?"

"That your whims are, in truth, quite varied," he answered, yawning.

The baroness indulged her whim with great energy. She immediately asked the girl if she would like to go to the city with her and, not even waiting for her answer, engaged her at once in her service, rechristened her Marietta, described in brilliant colors the position of a lady's maid, and, at the end, made her a present of a pair of slightly worn slippers and a coquettish house cap.

Old Foltýn was fairly numbed with joyous surprise when Marianka, with the great news, returned to him. Even in his dreams he would not have thought that his daughter would be chosen by fate to become the glittering pendant to that footman of whose relationship the entire Foltýn family boasted. Instantly he forgot the incident of the drum, his gait became sturdier and his eyes glowed like a youth's.

Several days passed. The baroness continued enthusiastic about the delights of country life and devoted herself with great eagerness to the education of Marietta as a lady's maid. Marietta often stood in front of the mirror wearing the coquettish cap and holding in her soft hand the large tuft of many-colored feathers which the mistress had purchased for her for brushing off the dust. Often, too, she sat on the low stool, her eyes gazing dreamily somewhere into the distance where in imagination she saw tall buildings, beautifully dressed people, and splendid equipages. Frequently she would bury her head in her hands and lose herself in deep thought. The baron would sit idly in the easy-chair, smoking and yawning. The steward and his wife rid themselves of all fears of their eminent guests. Beruška made friends with the purple footman playing "Twenty-six" with him in the office behind closed doors when they lighted their pipes.

Once towards evening the baroness, with her beautifully bound "Burns," stepped out into the flower-covered arbor in the park from which place there was a distant and varied view and where she hoped to await the nightingale concert which for several evenings had echoed in the neighborhood of the castle. The baron rebuked the footman for his fatness and ordered him to begin reducing by taking a walk out into the fields. The steward and his wife were putting up fruit behind closed doors. Melanie had a toothache.

In this idyllic, peaceful moment it occurred to old Foltýn that Marianka was lingering an unusually long time in the apartments of the nobility. He disposed of the thought, but it returned soon again. The thought became every moment more and more obtrusive.

"What is she doing there so long?" he growled into his moustaches. "The mistress is not in the house."

Involuntarily he went into the gallery and walked about a while, listening intently to sounds from above.

FOLTÝN'S DRUM

Then he ventured on the steps, urged by an irresistible force. On tiptoes he reached the corridor of the first floor. He stole to the footman's door and pressed the knob. It was closed. He crept to the door of the reception-room. Suddenly he paused. Within could be heard a voice—the voice of the baron. Distinctly he heard these words: "Don't be childish! Foolish whims! The world is different from what the priests and your simple-minded parents have painted it for you. I will make you happy. Whatever you wish, you will get—beautiful clothes, jewels, money—all. I will make your father a butler, steward, maybe even something higher. You will be in the city yourself. Now, my little dove, don't be ashamed, lift up your lovely eyes. God knows I never saw more beautiful ones!"

Foltýn stood as if thunderstruck. All the blood receded from his face. Horror and fright were depicted in it. He stooped down to the keyhole. Within he beheld the baron wholly changed. In his pale, handsome countenance there was not a single trace of sleepiness, and his dark eyes flashed with passion underneath the thin, proud brows. Uplifting by the chin Marianka's beautiful face, flushed deep scarlet with shame, he gazed lustfully upon her heaving bosom. Her eyes were cast down, in one hand she held the statuette, in the other the tousled tuft of variegated feathers.

Foltýn put his hands up to his gray head. Anguish

contracted his throat. Through his head rushed a whirl of terrible thoughts. Already he had reached for the door-knob, then quickly jerked his hand away. No! To have the baron learn that Marianka's father had listened to his words, to stand, shamed, and apprehended in an abominable deed before his own servant —no, that must not be! All of Foltýn's inborn loyalty rose in opposition. But what was he to do?

In the office was the footman. He would send him upstairs on some pretext. No sooner thought of than he hastened down. But the office was closed and perfect silence reigned within. Beruška and the footman who had but recently been playing cards inside were not at home. One was in the courtyard, the other out for a health promenade.

In desperation Foltýn ran down the corridor. Suddenly he paused in front of the jail-room. He stood but a moment and then burst open the door, seized the immense drum hanging there, hung it over his shoulder and ran out into the driveway. Wildly he swung the drumsticks, bowed his head, and then a deafening rattle resounded. He beat the drum until beads of sweat stood out on his brow.

The steward, hearing the clatter, turned as pale as death. "In God's name, Foltýn has gone mad," he burst out. He flew to the driveway. There he beheld Beruška, holding a card hand of spades in one hand and the collar of the unsummoned drummer in the other.

FOLTÝN'S DRUM

"Are you drunk?" shouted the clerk.

Foltýn continued obstinately to beat the drum. From all sides figures came running in the dusk.

The steward came to Beruška's assistance. "Stop, you maniac!" he thundered at Foltýn. "Don't you know the baron is already sleeping? I'll drive you out of service immediately."

"Oh, just let him stay in service," sounded the voice of the baron behind them. "He is a capital drummer." Then he passed through the bowing crowd, whistling and switching his riding-boots with his whip. He was going for a walk.

When the baroness, attracted hither by the mysterious sound of the drum, had returned from the nightingales' concert and entered the reception-room she beheld in the middle of it her beautiful, beloved statuette broken into many bits. From the weeping eyes of Marietta whom she summoned before her she at once learned the perpetrator. In great wrath she dismissed her from service on the spot. Short was the dream of tall buildings, beautiful people and splendid equipages!

At noon of the next day Foltýn stood in front of the castle and drummed the peasants to their labors. At the same time he gazed towards the forest road down which the noble carriage with marvelous speed was receding into the distance. When the carriage disappeared in the forest Foltýn breathed a sigh of relief, dropped the drumsticks and shook his head. And then the thought came into his head that, like the drum, he no longer belonged to the present era of the world. As to the cause of the disturbance of the day before he preserved an obstinate silence unto the day of his death.

JAN NERUDA

(Born July 10, 1834, in Malá Strana, Prague. Died Aug. 22, 1891, in Prague.)

THE childhood of Jan Neruda was spent in the vicinity of Ujezd barracks and later in humble quarters below the Royal Castle of Hradčany. He was exposed to all the privations of extreme poverty. He attended the school of St. Vít and the Malá Strana (Small Side) German school, and then entered the gymnasium, where he remained till he was sixteen. But inspired by a desire to study the Czech language and literature he entered the academic gymnasium, later taking up law and philosophy at the University. When but a youth of twenty his poem, "Oběšenec" (The Hanged Man), was accepted and published. This started him on a newspaper and literary career, and three years later his first book, "Hřbitovní Kvítí" (Churchyard Blossoms), appeared. Neruda for a while after his graduation was an instructor in private schools, but he soon returned to journalism and became editor successively of several noteworthy publications patronized by the younger writers of Bohemia. Some of his best feuilletons were written for the "Národní Listy" and were fortunately preserved as examples of his keen wit, kindly humor, and purposeful and valuable literary and dramatic criticism. In fact he stands as the founder of the feuilleton in his own country, establishing through his wide culture a standard for that class of writing far above any of his contemporaries in France and Germany.

The sorrow he experienced through the death of a beautiful woman whom he loved, he tried to forget in numerous trips to foreign lands, memories of which he has left in his superb sketches from Vienna, Istria, Dalmatia and other Balkan states, Italy, Constantinople, Egypt, Palestine, France, Germany. Later he wrote short stories, sketches and criticisms until the illness which had been creeping on him for years made further literary work impossible.

Ever since the publication of his first book of poems, Neruda has had a field of his own in his frank confessions, tinged with irony and temperate, cold scepticism not typical of youth. His second work, "A Book of Verses," was received with far more favor by a public which was now keener in its appreciation. Some of the poems in this collection, such as his "Lines to My Mother," have become national lyrics and ballads. His "Kosmické Písně" (Cosmic Songs) are at times simple lyrics, again reverent national hymns with here and there the genuinely earnest longings of a great soul to humanize the mysteries of the universe and make its workings more intimate by an analogy between the fate of little nations and of great powers, as in the case of Bohemia and its military neighbors, and in comparing the tragedies and joys of our earthly life as individuals with the course of the planets.

Neruda's "Ballady a Romance" (Ballads and Romances) is almost wholly devoted to his own nation and people. The poems in his "Prosté Motivy" (Simple Motives) are arranged according to the four seasons of the year which inspired the thoughts on nature and are the most exquisite contribution to literary impressionism in the Czech language. His last poetic collection, "Zpěvy Páteční" (Friday Songs), voices a deep consciousness of allegiance to a nation great in its ideals, yet greater in its sanctified sufferings and sacrifices.

Neruda produced one tragedy, "Francesca di Rimini," and several light comedies, which latter have been popular. In fact, certain of these comedies were reprinted from memory and produced in trenches or in camps by the Czechoslovak soldiers who for over five years have been in Russia and Siberia.

There is a freedom and independence in his realism which makes his figures as clear-cut as medallions. They are usually characters in his own intimately known Prague, some of them drawn exclusively from types known in his boyhood home, as in "Povidky Malostranské" (Small Side Tales) and others from the wider Prague in "Pražské Obrázky (Prague Pictures) and "Různí Lidé" (Various Sorts of People). Social problems are laid open to the very quick in

"Trhani" (The Mob), whereas in some of his briefer stories there is the charm of contrast between elegiac sorrows and dainty touches of humor. The big human heart of Neruda never permits him to despise his types or individuals, be they ever so unworthy as far as virtue or strength of character is concerned. He tells the story of each with just a touch of mother-sadness for the pathos of it all.

The story "He Was a Rascal" is, in considerable degree, autobiographical. His close knowledge of stage life through many years devoted to dramatic criticism is shown in the little sketch entitled "Beneš," in which the grief of that character is for the real Sontagova who died of Mexican fever while on a tour of the western continent. His "At the Sign of the Three Lilies" is rather a daring piece of realistic writing. In "The Vampire" he wastes no more words than would O. Henry but his artistry is the more exquisitely apparent.

THE VAMPIRE

BY JAN NERUDA

The excursion steamer brought us from Constantinople to the shore of the island of Prinkipo and we disembarked. The number of passengers was not large. There was one Polish family, a father, a mother, a daughter and her bridegroom, and then we two. Oh yes, I must not forget that when we were already on the wooden bridge which crosses the Golden Horn to Constantinople a Greek, a rather youthful man, joined us. He was probably an artist, judging by the portfolio he carried under his arm. Long black locks floated to his shoulders, his face was pale, and his black eyes were deeply set in their sockets. In the first moment he interested me, especially for his obligingness and for his knowledge of local conditions. But he talked too much, and I then turned away from him.

All the more agreeable was the Polish family. The father and mother were good-natured, fine people, the lover a handsome young fellow, of direct and refined manners. They had come to Prinkipo to spend the summer months for the sake of the daughter, who was slightly ailing. The beautiful pale girl was either just recovering from a severe illness or else a serious disease was just fastening its hold upon her. She leaned upon her lover when she walked and very often sat down to rest, while a frequent dry little cough interrupted her whispers. Whenever she coughed, her escort would considerately pause in their walk. He always cast upon her a glance of sympathetic suffering and she would look back at him as if she would say: "It is nothing. I am happy!" They believed in health and happiness.

On the recommendation of the Greek, who departed from us immediately at the pier, the family secured quarters in the hotel on the hill. The hotel-keeper was a Frenchman and his entire building was equipped comfortably and artistically, according to the French style.

We breakfasted together and when the noon heat had abated somewhat we all betook ourselves to the heights, where in the grove of Siberian stone-pines we could refresh ourselves with the view. Hardly had we found a suitable spot and settled ourselves when the Greek appeared again. He greeted us lightly, looked about and seated himself only a few steps from us. He opened his portfolio and began to sketch.

"I think he purposely sits with his back to the rocks so that we can't look at his sketch," I said.

"We don't have to," said the young Pole. "We have enough before us to look at." After a while he added, "It seems to me he's sketching us in as a sort of background. Well—let him!"

THE VAMPIRE

We truly did have enough to gaze at. There is not a more beautiful or more happy corner in the world than that very Prinkipo! The political martyr, Irene, contemporary of Charles the Great, lived there for a month as an exile. If I could live a month of my life there I would be happy for the memory of it for the rest of my days! I shall never forget even that one day spent at Prinkipo.

The air was as clear as a diamond, so soft, so caressing, that one's whole soul swung out upon it into the distance. At the right beyond the sea projected the brown Asiatic summits; to the left in the distance purpled the steep coasts of Europe. The neighboring Chalki, one of the nine islands of the "Prince's Archipelago," rose with its cypress forests into the peaceful heights like a sorrowful dream, crowned by a great structure—an asylum for those whose minds are sick.

The Sea of Marmora was but slightly ruffled and played in all colors like a sparkling opal. In the distance the sea was as white as milk, then rosy, between the two islands a glowing orange and below us it was beautifully greenish blue, like a transparent sapphire. It was resplendent in its own beauty. Nowhere were there any large ships—only two small craft flying the English flag sped along the shore. One was a steamboat as big as a watchman's booth, the second had about twelve oarsmen and when their oars rose simultaneously molten silver dripped from them. Trustful dolphins darted in and out among them and dove with long, arching flights above the surface of the water. Through the blue heavens now and then calm eagles winged their way, measuring the space between two continents.

The entire slope below us was covered with blossoming roses whose fragrance filled the air. From the coffee-house near the sea music was carried up to us through the clear air, hushed somewhat by the distance.

The effect was enchanting. We all sat silent and steeped our souls completely in the picture of paradise. The young Polish girl lay on the grass with her head supported on the bosom of her lover. The pale oval of her delicate face was slightly tinged with soft color, and from her blue eyes tears suddenly gushed forth. The lover understood, bent down and kissed tear after tear. Her mother also was moved to tears, and I—even I—felt a strange twinge.

"Here mind and body both must get well," whispered the girl. "How happy a land this is!"

"God knows I haven't any enemies, but if I had I would forgive them here!" said the father in a trembling voice.

And again we became silent. We were all in such a wonderful mood—so unspeakably sweet it all was! Each felt for himself a whole world of happiness and each one would have shared his happiness with the whole world. All felt the same—and so no one disturbed another. We had scarcely even noticed that the Greek, after an hour or so, had arisen, folded his

THE VAMPIRE

portfolio and with a slight nod had taken his departure. We remained.

Finally after several hours, when the distance was becoming overspread with a darker violet, so magically beautiful in the south, the mother reminded us it was time to depart. We arose and walked down towards the hotel with the easy elastic steps that characterize carefree children. We sat down in the hotel under the handsome veranda.

Hardly had we been seated when we heard below the sounds of quarrelling and oaths. Our Greek was wrangling with the hotel-keeper, and for the entertainment of it we listened.

The amusement did not last long. "If I didn't have other guests," growled the hotel-keeper, and ascended the steps towards us.

"I beg you to tell me, sir," asked the young Pole of the approaching hotel-keeper, "who is that gentleman? What is his name?"

"Eh—who knows what the fellow's name is?" grumbled the hotel-keeper, and he gazed venomously downwards. "We call him the Vampire."

"An artist?"

"Fine trade! He sketches only corpses. Just as soon as someone in Constantinople or here in the neighborhood dies, that very day he has a picture of the dead one completed. That fellow paints them beforehand—and he never makes a mistake—just like a vulture!"

The old Polish woman shrieked affrightedly. In her arms lay her daughter pale as chalk. She had fainted.

In one bound the lover had leaped down the steps. With one hand he seized the Greek and with the other reached for the portfolio.

We ran down after him. Both men were rolling in the sand. The contents of the portfolio were scattered all about. On one sheet, sketched with a crayon, was the head of the young Polish girl, her eyes closed and a wreath of myrtle on her brow.

BENEŠ

BY JAN NERUDA

IN a certain little wine-shop near the Carinthian theatre in Vienna it was usually lively, day in and day out, but today, laughter and shouts filled the entire side-street. This was the meeting-place of the singers and chorus girls of the court opera and of the members of the orchestra, all of them people free from every care, for if they had admitted the first care they would then have had to admit altogether too many. The less of sweetness life offered them the more feverishly they rushed into it.

Even old gray Beneš, usually morose and short spoken, was as if transformed today. He drank, talked, drank and talked again. His expressive face was already flushed and was covered with a perpetual smile. His classic cape, in winter and in summer always the same, hung behind him on a hook, but the old man felt the fire of the wine and had already removed his vest also. It struck no one as freakish that underneath the first vest of heavy material there appeared a second thick vest. They were thoroughly acquainted with Beneš and knew all of his peculiarities.

Beneš had been an accompanist and rehearser of

operas for some forty years. The wider musical circles knew him as an excellent reader of parts, the inner circles knew him as a happy composer of delightful little lyrics, and all recognized in him an all-around good fellow, a little peevish, to be sure, but always willing to make concessions. Therefore, only to the lighter-minded ones of the company did his vivaciousness seem unsuspicious. The others surmised that it was probably more of a cloak, that Beneš talked constantly in order to silence something and that he drank much to drown much. These said nothing but they, too, were gay.

"Aha—our Leon! I was sure you'd come in today!" called Beneš to a new-comer. He was a young man of quick actions, merry face and shrewd glance. Willingly they prepared a place for him.

"Leon is a lion," said some one in the rear. "Daddy Beneš, did you hear Leo today in church?"

"You fellows would teach me to know him!" Beneš puffed up and the second vest was flung off. Under it appeared a third vest. "You dare to tell me what any one's worth is! Better keep still! Leo will be a second Ronconi—Ronconi was also as small and with a voice like a thunderous flute. You people have heard a lot in life! If I say that someone will really amount to something, they will! I've foretold to this little minx here that she will be as happy and as famous as—as Sontag." This name slipped from his lips as if by accident.

"What's that Daddy Beneš is saying?" a pretty, merry-faced young girl, sitting near him, asked in German.

"Oh, nothing, minx," said he, patting her hair. "What's new in Zlonits, Leon?"

"Nothing for a long time, nothing at all! But, thunder!—Daddy has a new cravat today." Beneš consciously drew his chin up high and stretched out his legs. "And look at his finely polished boots, too. Daddy is celebrating something today!"

Beneš frowned slightly. "Don't crowd up so close to me, Pauline." And he turned again to the young girl.

"Lukova is taking a shine to Daddy!" was the cry from around the circle.

"Daddy, haven't you got some new songs for me?" asked the young chorus girl, destined later to become a renowned prima donna.

Beneš paused to look at her. "You are pretty—but you haven't such eyes as hers, after all! Well, it's all one, you'll amount to something—you and Leon here—but the rest won't get very far!"

"Oho—who can know that?" wrathfully exclaimed a young violinist opposite. "You, too, had talent, Daddy, well—and—" He did not finish.

"Well, and what? What could an accompanist become other than an accompanist? I was one in Prague and I am the same in Vienna."

"But what if you had finished your studies in Prague?"

"Yes—if! If I hadn't run off to Vienna after Henrietta Sontag!"

"She must have been beautiful, wasn't she?"

"I don't even know that, absolutely," burst forth Beneš with a lightness that was plainly feigned. "She was and she wasn't. When I met her by accident in a Prague company I accompanied her on the piano for the first time and when she looked at me, all was over. Dear God, those blue eyes of hers! I would have followed those eyes further than Vienna!"

No one questioned him further, but Beneš, nevertheless, did not remain silent. It seemed as if something goaded him on to speaking jocularly and lightly of that subject.

"It didn't even worry me that others also had come here on her account—a young lancer, for instance. I knew she was as pure as an angel. Dear God, those eyes so soft, so heavenly! Why shouldn't I say so now? What does it matter? I was insanely in love with her and I acted like a madman. I kept silent. She herself cured me. Suddenly she disappeared—it was said, on account of attacks from certain court circles on her virtue—and for me she left this written message, 'I thank you fervently for your services and please accept enclosed three hundred as a reward for your difficult work of accompaniment.' So then at last I saw what I was to her—an accompanist! But for the first time in my life I had three hundred and—"

He intended to say something humorous, but suddenly became silent. His whole body trembled as if he were shaking with the ague, his face suddenly became rigid, his eye was fixed on the floor, his lips remained open. His folded hands quivered convulsively.

"And when did she die of that Mexican cholera—it can't be so many years ago?" asked a close neighbor, speaking perhaps only to keep the conversation going.

"On the eleventh of June, 1854," answered Beneš in a lifeless tone.

"The eleventh—why today it is just exactly—"

Beneš's head sank down on his clasped hands. Within the room a sudden stillness followed, no one speaking a word. It was a painful silence, broken only by the old man's audible, unspeakably heartbreaking sobbing.

For a long while the old man's weeping continued, no one uttering even a whisper.

Suddenly the sobbing ceased. The old man raised himself and covered his eyes with his palm.

"Good night!" he said almost in a whisper and staggered towards the door.

AT THE SIGN OF THE THREE LILIES

BY JAN NERUDA

I THINK I must have been insane that time. Every fibre of my being was alive, my blood was at a white heat.

It was a warm, but dark, summer night. The sulphurous, dead air of the last few days had finally rolled itself up into black clouds. The stormy wind had whipped them before it earlier in the evening, then the mighty tempest burst its fury, a heavy shower came crashing down and the storm and rain lasted late into the night.

I was sitting under the wooden arcade of the hotel called "At the Sign of the Three Lilies" near the Strahov Gate. It was a small inn, which in those times always had more numerous visitors on Sundays when, in the main room the cadets and corporals used to enjoy themselves dancing to the strains of a piano.

Today it was Sunday. I sat under the arcades at a table close to the window, all alone. The mighty peals of thunder roared almost in constant succession, the downpour beat upon the tile roof above me, the water

AT THE SIGN OF THE THREE LILIES

drizzling in splattering streams to the ground, while the piano inside the main room had only brief intervals of rest, ever bursting into sound anew. At times I looked through the open door at the whirling, laughing couples, and again I would gaze out into the dark garden. Sometimes when a brighter streak of lightning flashed I could see near the garden wall at the end of the arcade white piles of human bones. Formerly there had been a small burying-ground here and this very week they had dug up the skeletons from it in order to rebury them elsewhere. The ground was still torn up and the graves were open.

However, I was able to remain at my table only a little while each time. Often I would arise and approach for a moment the wide-open door of the main saloon to have a closer look at the dancers. Each time I was attracted by a lovely girl of about eighteen years of age. Of slender figure, of full warm outlines, with loose black hair, cut just to the neck, an oval, smooth face, and bright eyes, she was indeed a beautiful young girl. Her eyes enchanted me. Liquid clear they were, as mysterious as the calm surface of water, yet so restless, recalling to you at once the words, "Sooner will a fire be satiated with wood and the sea with water than a beautiful-eyed maid will be satiated with men!"

She danced almost constantly. But well she observed that she had attracted my gaze. Whenever she danced past the door in which I stood she would fasten her eyes on me, and as she danced on further into the hall I saw and felt that at every turn she bent her eye on me. I did not notice her talking to anyone during the course of the evening.

Again I stood there. Our eyes met immediately, although the girl stood in the very last row. The quadrille was nearing its close, the fifth round was just being finished, when another girl entered the hall, all out of breath and dripping wet. She forced her way to the girl with the beautiful eyes. The musicians were just striking up the sixth set. While the first chain was being formed, the new-comer whispered something to the girl with the lovely eyes and the latter nodded her head silently. The sixth set lasted somewhat longer, a brisk young cadet calling the changes. When it came to an end, the beautiful girl glanced once more towards the door leading into the garden, then went to the front door of the hall. I could see her as she slipped out, covering her head with her outer garments and then she vanished.

I went and sat down again at my place. The storm began anew as if it had not even begun to show its fury. The wind howled with renewed strength, the lightnings flashed. I listened shiveringly, but thought only of the girl, of those wondrous eyes of hers. To go home now was not, of course, to be even seriously thought of.

After a quarter of an hour I again glanced towards the door of the dancing-hall. There again stood the

AT THE SIGN OF THE THREE LILIES

girl with the enchanting eyes. She was arranging her wet garments, drying her damp hair, while some older girl companion helped her.

"Why did you go home in such foul weather?" she asked.

"My sister came for me." I heard her voice for the first time. It was silkily soft and musical.

"Did something happen at home?"

"My mother just died."

My whole body quivered.

The lovely eyed girl turned and stepped outside into the solitude. She stood near me, her eyes rested on mine. I felt her fingers close to my trembling hand. I seized her hand—it was so soft and tender.

Silently I drew the girl farther and farther into the arcade and she followed freely.

The storm had now reached its height. The wind rushed like a surging flood, heaven and earth roared, above our heads the thunders rolled, and all around us it was as if the dead were shrieking from their graves.

She pressed close to me. I felt her damp clothing clinging to my breast. I felt her soft body, her warm glowing breath—I felt that I must drink out that depraved soul from the very depths of her being!

HE WAS A RASCAL

BY JAN NERUDA

HORÁČEK was dead. Nobody regretted his death, for they knew him throughout all of Small Side.[1] In Small Side people know their neighbors well, perhaps because they know no one else, and when Horáček died they told each other it was a good thing, for by his death his good mother would be relieved, and then, "He was a rascal." He died in the twenty-fifth year of his age, suddenly, as was stated in the obituary lists. In that list his character was not entered, for the reason, as the chief clerk in the drugstore very wittily remarked, that a rascal really has no character. But how different it would have been if the chief clerk had died! Nobody knew a thing against or about him! Horáček's corpse was hauled out with other corpses from the public chapel. "As was his life, so was his end," said the chief clerk in the drugstore. Behind the carriage walked a small group, composed mainly of persons in somewhat holiday attire, and therefore all the more noticeably beggars.

[1] Small Side, "Malá Strana," is a part of the city of Prague, connected with the Old Town by means of the stone bridge of King Charles erected in 1357.

HE WAS A RASCAL

In the group only two persons properly belonged to Horáček's funeral procession, his aged mother and a very elegantly dressed young man who supported her. He was very pale, his gait was oddly trembling and uncertain, indeed it seemed at times as if he shook with chills. The Small Side populace scarcely noticed the weeping mother, for her burden was now lightened, and though she wept it was just because she was a mother and doubtless from joy. The young man, however, was in all probability from some other quarter, for no one recognized him.

"Poor fellow! He himself needs to be supported! Most likely he attended the funeral on Mrs. Horáček's account!—What's that? A friend of young Horáček's? —Why, who would publicly acknowledge friendship for the disgraced man? Besides, Horáček from childhood had no friends. He was always a rascal! Unhappy mother!"

The mother cried heartbreakingly all the way and great tears rolled down the young man's cheeks, despite the fact that Horáček had been a rascal from his very childhood.

Horáček's parents were hucksters. They did not fare ill as, in general, hucksters who have their own shop get along well where many poor people live. Money gathers slowly, to be sure, when it comes in by kreutzers and groats for wood, butter and lard, especially when one must throw in a pinch of salt and caraway. But for all that, the groats are cash and two-groat debts were punctually paid. Besides, Mrs. Horáček had patrons among the officials' wives, and they praised her fine butter. They took a good deal of it, for they did not pay till the first of the month.

Their boy, František, was already nearly three years old and still wore girl's dresses. The neighbor women said he was an ugly child. The neighbors' children were older and seldom did František become emboldened enough to play with them. Once the children were calling names after a passing Jew. František was among them, but he was not crying out. The Jew started at a run after the children and caught František, who did not even attempt to run away. With curses the Jew led him to his parents. The neighbor women were shocked that the homely little František was already a rascal.

His mother was frightened and took counsel with her husband.

"I shall not beat him, but here at home he would grow wild among the children, for we can't look after him. Let us put him in a nursery!"

František was put into trousers and went with lamentation to the nursery school. He sat there for two years. The first year he received as a reward for his quietness at the annual examination a breakfast roll. The second year he would have gotten a little picture if things hadn't been spoiled for him. The day before the examination he was going home at noon. He had to go past the house of a rich landholder. In front of the house poultry used to run through the quiet street, and František often enjoyed himself heartily with them. That day there were on promenade a number of turkey hens which František had never seen before in his life. He stood still and gazed at them in rapture. Ere long, František was squatting down among them and was carrying on important discourses with them. He forgot about his dinner and about school, and when the children at the afternoon session told that František was playing with the turkey hens instead of going to school the schoolmaster sent the school maid-servant to bring him. At the examination František received nothing, and the schoolmaster told his mother to attend to him more severely, that he was already a regular rascal.

And in reality František was a thorough rascal. In the parish school he sat beside the son of the inspector and used to go home with him, hand in hand. They used to play together at the inspector's house. František was permitted to rock the youngest child, and for that he would get a little white pot of coffee for lunch. The inspector's son always had beautiful clothes and a white, stiffly starched collar. František wore clean clothes, to be sure, but they were abundantly patched. For that matter, it never occurred to him that he was dressed any differently than the inspector's son. One day after school the teacher paused beside the two boys, patted the inspector's son on the cheek and said: "See, Conrad, what a fine boy you are, for you can keep your collar from getting soiled! Give my cordial greetings to your respected father!"

"Yes, sir," answered František.

"I'm not talking to you, you piece of patchwork!"

František could not see at once why his patches made impossible a message of greeting from the teacher to his father, but he began suspecting that there was, after all, some sort of difference between himself and the inspector's son, so he gave the latter a good thrashing. He was driven out as an irredeemable rascal.

His parents sent him to the German schools. František scarcely understood a single word of German, and consequently progressed very miserably in his studies. His teachers regarded him as a careless fellow, although he surely toiled enough. They considered his morals spoiled, because he always defended himself when the boys shoved into him, and he was unable to give any explanation in German of the reason for his scuffles. The boys in reality had plenty to tease him about. Every little while he made some laughable mistake in German and in other ways furnished causes for derisive diversion. Their chief amusement, however, was occasioned one day when he arrived at school wearing a quilted green cap with a horizontal shade as thick as one's finger, standing out from it. His father had purposely made a trip to the Old Town to select something special for him.

"This won't break and neither will the sun burn you,"

HE WAS A RASCAL

he said, after sewing on the shade, and František really thought he had something unusually ornamental and strutted proudly to school. Endless laughter greeted him, the boys hopped about him, assuring him that his shade was, compared to other shades, like a side post among thin planks, and they called him the "jamb boy." František broke the nose of one of the boys with his "jamb," for which he got the lowest grade in deportment, and had all he could do later to be accepted into the gymnasium.

His parents wished to make every effort to have their son become somebody so that he would not be compelled to earn his bread by as hard means as they did. The teachers and neighbors tried to talk them out of the notion, saying he had no ability, and besides that, he was a rascal. Indeed, among the neighbors he had that reputation. He was particularly unfortunate with them, although in reality he did no more than their own children, possibly even less. Whenever he played ball on the street it was sure to fly into someone's open window and when with his companions he played at shuttlecock in the driveway he was sure to break the lamp under the cross, although he took pains to be careful.

Nevertheless František, who was now called Horáček, entered the gymnasium. It cannot be said that he applied himself to school studies with excessive perseverance, for they had begun to disgust him when he was in the German school. His general progress was only enough to permit him to advance year after year without much difficulty to the next higher division. But for that Horáček studied all the more fervently those subjects which do not strictly belong in school. He read diligently whatever came into his hands, and very soon had a thorough knowledge of literature in foreign tongues. His German style was soon very polished. It was the only subject in which he received a grade of "excellent" throughout his career at the gymnasium. His exercises were always replete with beautiful thoughts and phrases. His teacher once asserted that he had a style so flowery that it resembled Herder's style. They had regard for this, and when he did not know much in other branches they would say that he had great talent, but that he was a rascal. They did not, however, trust themselves to spoil his talent and Horáček slipped through even the final decisive examination.

He became a law student, as was the custom and also because his father wished him to become an official. Horáček now had even more time for reading, and because, at this time, he fell happily in love he himself began to write. The papers published his first attempts, and all of Small Side was immeasurably exasperated that he had become a literary man and that he wrote for the papers and, what was worst of all, for the Czech papers. They prophesied that he would now rapidly go to the dogs, and when, after a short time, his father died they knew with certainty that he had grieved himself to death over his rascally son.

His mother gave up the huckster business. After a short time things went hard with them and Horáček had to see to it that he earned something. He could not give private instruction, and then, too, no one wanted him as a private teacher. He would have liked to look around for some small official position, but he had not yet decided. A taste for further study would not have hindered, law was a distasteful enough fare, and he attended college only when time hung on his hands. At the beginning of his law studies he made a resolution that for every hour he attended lectures he would write an epigram. He began with antique distichs, but when he read his first written epigram he saw that his hexameter had seven feet. He had much joy of his new meter and he determined to write only in heptameters. When, however, he thought of publishing them, he counted his heptameters and discovered they had expanded to eight.

His chief obstacle was his love affair. The young girl, beautiful and truly lovable, was filled with a pure, strong love for him, and her parents did not force her to consider any one else, although there were suitors in plenty for her hand. The girl wished to wait for Horáček until after he had finished his studies and had secured a good place. The official position which was offered to Horáček had the advantage of an immediate salary but there were no prospects of advancement in the future. Horáček knew well that the girl he loved would have no future with him. He could not sacrifice her to a life of privations. He thought he was much less in love with her than he really was and he resolved to give her up. He had not the heart to renounce her in a direct manner. He wished to be repulsed, driven away. It was an unconscious desire to revel in undeserved pain. A means of accomplishing his end soon occurred to him. He wrote an anonymous letter in a disguised hand, relating the most shameful things about himself and sent the letter to the parents of the girl he loved. The girl would not believe the informer, but her father was more worldly wise, made inquiries of Horáček's neighbors and heard from them that the young man had been a rascal from youth. When Horáček came to make a call a few days later, the weeping girl ran into another room and he was politely driven out of the house. The young girl became a bride not long after, and the rumor spread throughout Small Side that Horáček had been banished from the house for his rascality.

Now, indeed, Horáček's heart ached to the breaking-point. He had lost the only person who truly loved him, and he could not deny that it was through his own fault. He lost courage, his new occupation proved distasteful to him and he began to languish and fail visibly. His neighbors were not in the least surprised, for, said they, it was the natural consequence of reckless living.

HE WAS A RASCAL

His present work was in a private banking-house. Despite his dislike for it, he worked industriously, and his employer soon placed entire confidence in him, even entrusting large sums of money to him when these had to be delivered somewhere. Horáček also had an opportunity to earn the gratitude of his employer's son. One day the young man waited for Horáček when the latter was just departing.

"Mr. Horáček, if you will not help me, I shall have to drown myself and cause my father disgrace in order to escape my own shame. I owe a debt which must absolutely be paid today. I shall not receive my own money until day after tomorrow and I don't know what to do. You are delivering some money to my uncle—. Entrust it to me for the time being and day after tomorrow everything will be fully settled. Uncle will not ask father about the money!"

But the uncle did ask, and the next day this notice appeared in the newspapers: "I request all who have any dealings with me to entrust no money to František Horáček. I have discharged him on account of dishonesty." Even a report of a fire in some other quarter would not have interested Small Side so much as did this.

Horáček did not betray the son of his employer. He went home and lay down in bed under the pretext that he had a headache.

The district doctor for the poor on the following day

entered the drugstore at his regular hour, somewhat absorbed in thought.

"So, then, that rascal is dead?" asked the clerk suddenly.

"Horáček?—Well, yes!"

"And what did he die of?"

"Well, now—perhaps we'll say in the records that he was stricken with apoplexy."

"So! Well, after all, it's a good thing that he didn't run up a lot of bills for medicines, the rascal!"

FRANTIŠEK XAVIER SVOBODA

(Born October 25, 1860, in Moníšek.)

THE love of out-of-doors, due to his country birth and bringing up, breathes through each of Svoboda's stories even when they concern themselves with the life of the effete and those whose interests are far from those of nature. Svoboda's technical education in the substantial realities of every-day life prepared him for a position as official in the city bank in Prague, where he remained until 1911, but it did not crush out of him appreciation and love for all that nature gives so generously.

Mr. Svoboda has been almost equally active along three lines of literary expression:—as a poet, as a dramatist and as a novelist and short-story writer.

His early activities were in the line of poetical production, the first fruits being his "Básně" (Poems) of 1883–85. More keen and far deeper are his later collections—"Nálady z Minulých Let" (Moods of Former Years), 1890, and "Květy Z Mých Lučin" (Blossoms from My Meadows), 1891. Other books of lyrics and epics have followed since that time.

As a dramatist, few modern writers excel him in realism, verisimilitude and character delineation.

The dramas, "Márinka Válkova" and "Olga Rubešova," both named for their leading female characters; "Rozklad" (Disintegration); "Směry Života" (Aims of Life); "Útok Zisku" (The Assault of Acquisition); "Podvracený Dub" (The Overthrown Oak); "Odpoutané Zlo" (The Unbound Evil); "Přes Tři Vrchy" (Over Three Mounts) and "Démon" (The Demon) reveal him as a profound psychologist. His best plays in lighter, but no less genuine, vein are his "Fialka" (The Violet); "Dědečku, dědečku" (Grandfather); "Rozveselená Rodina" (The Merry Family); "Lapený Samsonek" (Samson Made Captive); "Mlsáničko" (The Dainty Bit); and "Poupě" (The Bud).

It is Svoboda, the short-story writer, who effectively gives a cross-section of life as he knows it in various fields. The realism evident in his initial collection of "Povídky" (Stories), published almost as early as his first book of poems, holds his readers as strongly as his sketch "Probuzení" (The Awakening), which probes the soul of a student to its depths. The author is not always concerned with the social, national or philosophical significance of a deed, but is often the teller of a story for the story's own sake.

His scenes and characters are selected from all sorts and conditions of life and are usually objectively presented with much illuminating and lively dialogue. Among his very readable collections of stories are: "Náladové Povídky" (Stories of Moods), "Drobné

FRANTIŠEK XAVIER SVOBODA 103

Příhody" (Minor Incidents), "Pestré Povídky" (Motley Tales), "Z Brdských Lesů" (From the Brd Forests), "Válečné Sny Františka Poláka" (War Dreams of Frank Polák), "Vášeň a Osud" (Passion and Fate).

His brief romances, entitled "Srdce Její Vzkvétalo Vždy Dvěma Květy" (Her Heart Ever Bloomed with Two Blossoms) and "Až Ledy Poplují" (When the Ice Flows), have been very popular.

The ability of the author as a realist possessed of the keenest dramatic instinct, expressed by an art so great that it is wholly unapparent is shown in this simple tale of a soldier of the Hapsburg army "Every Fifth Man," is selected from his "War Dreams of Frank Polák."

EVERY FIFTH MAN

BY FRANTISEK X. SVOBODA

HALF of our company stood on a height near a heavy battery of cannon. I was with the other half which took its position among the furrows of a potato-field, a considerable distance from our main army, which for two hours had kept up a fusillade with the enemy infantry, thinly spread out beyond a swampy meadow, on a low green hill. In the potato-field among the yellowish, frosted stalks where we lay, chiefly as guard for observing the left flank, the smoke whitened every little while and a ball sped idly somewhere into the broad pasture land on the elevated ground, where the enemy soldiers looked like small, bluish, sparsely planted flowers in a green field.

A shot whistled past my ear and lost itself in the soft and, as yet, transparently clear air.

I was lying in a deep unraked ridge of pebbly loam, holding in my hand a loaded gun aimed straight ahead. I was not shooting. It seemed useless to me. The potato-vine was near my eyes and exhaled an odor of decaying leaves. I looked about over the country and everything that appeared before me in the broad picture pleased me. The view was unobstructed and the infrequent shooting of this section of the army suggested merely a maneuver, more than a real battle. One felt a certain pleasure and freedom in being in this low country, and it was not disagreeable to lie in the furrows. My eyes were delighted with the harmony of the lovely autumn colors which in all their shades and tints had touched everything in the level field as well as in the small distant forests.

In front of me lay the infantryman, Vaněk, a tall, bony fellow with an irregular, pale-colored full beard, but with a good-natured manner and a simple, open face. He usually remained aloof out of some sort of rural shyness, and meditated quietly on his own affairs. He was an older man, married and the father of three children, as I learned in conversation with him. The tips of his big boots with their broad soles were dug into the furrow and his trousers were soiled from the soft earth.

"We're well off here, aren't we, Vaněk?" I said to him.

"Well off is right, Mr. Sergeant," he answered readily. "Very comfortable."

"If it would only be like this every day we'd be happy, wouldn't we?"

"Well, I should say so! Ha! Ha!"

"Oh, as for our rustic," sounded the thin, disagreeable voice of another infantryman, Ejem, lying not far off, "he is right at home here!" (They always called Vaněk "the rustic.")

"He smells potatoes," Ejem continued, laughing. "If he could only pull up a few and take them to his wife!"

The others all laughed.

"Sure," calmly added Vaněk.

"Here, you're fairly rolling in potatoes, aren't you?" Ejem teased. "And when at home someone gives you a potato you don't know what it is and have to go to the neighbors to ask."

The soldiers burst out laughing anew. Vaněk growled out something, but later laughed with the rest.

Just then we caught a glimpse of Major Holay riding up to our division on his powerful horse, choosing his way along the slope of the hill so that the enemy shots could not reach him. The horse was going at a trot, his broad, smooth breast shining in the sunlight, while his lifted head tossed restlessly. From his mouth frothed white foam and his feet moved quickly through the air like black flexible metal rods. The Major's brown coat with its gold collar, his blue trousers and high boots were distinctly outlined in the center of the open spaces with their dark, autumnal coloring. We heard the hollow sound of the hoofs and the neighing of the horse, indeed it seemed to us that we heard even the smack of the Major's lips and the peculiar swish of his boots against the straps.

"The Major is coming!" cried Ejem, and we all felt a sudden fear.

Vaněk moved a little in trying to arrange himself to

lie as he had been taught in drill and as our service orders prescribed.

"On his raven-black steed he rides," continued Ejem in a singing and unnatural voice as he set his gun close to his face. "We must act as if we were shooting," he added, continuing to adjust himself.

The approaching Major Holay caused considerable stir among us, for his extreme severity was not at all in favor among the younger men of the army who were unused to the rigorous military service in which Holay, in former years, had grown up.

"Why is he coming here?" I thought to myself in fear, changing to a sort of feverishness. "Is it because we are lying here so comfortably and not firing much? He's certain to order us to lie some different way and do more shooting."

"Now then, fire! Fire away!" in muffled tones commanded Lieutenant Schuster who until now had said nothing. "In regular fashion—and give 'em plenty! Hufský, fire! Ejem, shoot! Polák, give heed!"

The shooting from our division in the potato-field echoed in frequent succession now, and into the air were carried innumerable puffs of white, smelling smoke. The observation and firing were now more alert as if we were Heaven knows how enthusiastic about this senseless fusillade. Major Holay had such an influence over us that we feared him and the majority of the soldiers hated him. His full, double-chinned milky white, shaved face, with its moustache and small

EVERY FIFTH MAN 109

side-whiskers, its large, sharp nose, closely compressed lips and half-closed eyes in their gray, half-concealing lashes was altogether too cold, cruel and disagreeable to win affection from anyone. He never smiled and always gazed off somewhere, shouting out at intervals his brusque orders in gruffly overbearing manner.

He was about six steps distant from us. We were now shooting copiously, keeping an eye on the Major meanwhile.

Suddenly a shot whizzed in a different direction than the rest. Immediately after we saw Major Holay leaning backward and about to fall from his horse.

"He is shot!" flashed through my brain, and a strange foreboding overpowered me.

"That was one of you!" furiously shrieked Schuster and leaped into the furrows where we were lying. His legs encased in knickerbockers were dark above me. A disagreeable chill went through my body.

No one answered. The Lieutenant's violent cry was carried through the clear autumn sunshine.

"Some one of you fellows here! Who was it?" he cried in a hoarse voice. "Who was it?" he shouted again with a kind of fierce agitation.

We looked silently at the Major as he sank from his horse. His huge body bent backwards. His cap fell off and one foot was for an instant caught in the stirrup. The horse reared up and in wild affright started running across the plain, whitened with stubble. The Major's body remained lying beside the road.

No one of us had yet uttered a word. The Lieutenant in the greatest excitement still shouted and scrutinized one gun after another. Every one was aimed in the direction of the enemy. We had ceased shooting and lay motionless. Deep emotion held back our breath. Schuster's black, fiery eyes glistened in his red face and fairly snapped flames at all of the prostrate soldiers.

"Who was it?" he screamed again, turning his face in the direction where lay our army.

I arose and placed myself directly in front of him. He was frightened.

"We cannot leave the Major lying there!" I said in a very earnest voice, looking into his glittering eyes. "He may be only wounded! We must go to his aid!" I spoke rapidly, looking about in alarm and forgetting all military precepts.

He was somewhat startled, amazed that I spoke suddenly of something altogether different from what he had, in the first instant, expected, and the fire in his eyes died down. A visible embarrassment took possession of him and he only babbled something indistinct into the air. Someone laughed, and this little burst of merriment incensed him anew.

"We must carry him away!" I said with definiteness.

"Yes, yes," he replied, absently. "We will carry him away, of course—we'll carry him away!" And he gazed around.

Immediately, at his command, his corporal with four

EVERY FIFTH MAN 111

men departed to carry away the corpse of Holay. We did no more firing. We looked continually in the direction in which they were bearing the Major. His horse galloping with flying mane disappeared somewhere near the road among the trees.

About an hour later the enemy infantry retired and our division returned to the main army. We went without a word, agitated and with misgivings. Constantly I saw in my mind's eye Major Holay, his severe, milky-pale face and his blinking eyes. Even a strange grief filled my being and to my mind there kept coming, along the way, affecting memories of various incidents experienced with Major Holay. At times I was convinced that Major Holay was in reality a good man and I said, finally, aloud, "He was misunderstood, misunderstood!"

Hardly had we rejoined our company when our Captain, with ruddy face, rode out on his horse. Schuster stepped forward and announced to him what had happened.

"I know," answered the Captain severely. "The shot came from our division. The bullet found in the breast of Major Holay is our bullet." Then he turned to us. "Who did it?" he asked, raising himself on his stout mare.

No one answered.

"Let him announce himself!" he shouted.

Absolute silence reigned in our ranks.

"As you know, in war there is no time for investigation. If you don't tell who did it, I'll order you all shot down!"

Lieutenant Schuster, standing beside the Captain, affected at these words a very stern mien, twisting his black moustaches.

"In five minutes," shouted the Captain, "you will again form ranks. I invite you to deliver up the scoundrel who killed the Major. If not, you will all be shot!" And, urging on his horse, he rode quickly away.

A great anxiety forced itself into my bosom. The Captain's words sounded forth sharply and icily. To my mind there came recollections of "articles" in times of war where it always stated, "He will be shot."

The soldiers now began to talk noisily.

"Not a word will they get out of us!" they vowed mutually.

"They won't do so very much to us!" said someone, and several others repeated the same opinion with emphasis. A sort of activity and excitement was now plainly noticeable in this division. All of them laughed. Only I felt anxious and depressed.

After a while the Captain rode up perspiring. He brought with him the orders of the Colonel. Seeing him, we became silent and looked at each other in sudden fear.

His face was angrily clouded, his full beard seemed to be grayer than usual and his actions were more de-

EVERY FIFTH MAN 113

termined and speedier. His stout horse kept rearing all the time and refused to quiet down. Among us, all laughter had quickly vanished. A grave mood fell on all when the Captain rode out before us and cried out, "Will you deliver up the criminal?"

His voice was icy, no longer as brawling as before, but more effective. I felt a chill from my feet clear to my head, and I looked around at the other men as if I expected that one of them would speak out. A deep, oppressive silence reigned.

The Captain then rode directly up to us and said something to Lieutenant Schuster, who, for reasons unknown to me, was flushing deeply. Then he lifted his head as high as possible and gave orders for us to stand in a single row, without regard to size or rank.

"Quickly! Quickly!" he shouted, seeing that the men stepped up to their neighbors with a sort of mistrust, slowness and fear.

As I passed Schuster he whispered to me, "Every fifth man—take care!"

Something immoderately, indefinably appalling fell on my chest. My heart began to beat wildly, the blood rushed to my head, and into my eyes a great heat poured. I could not at once comprehend the words of the Lieutenant and I pressed forward into the long row extending out in either direction. I found myself in the right wing, practically near the end of that long line, winding through the white oat stubble. I was without reflection, without any sort of clear conception, and I heard only as in a dream the shouting of the Captain, whose wide trousers on his massive legs were constantly before my eyes.

"Hurry quickly! Quickly!" he cried. "Into line! Into line!"

Of a sudden, a clear beam penetrated my brain. "Every fifth man," sounded in my ears, and I comprehended the confidential message of Lieutenant Schuster.

"Every fifth man will be shot," I whispered to myself. Oppressed with agony, I quickly counted from the right end. I was the tenth man. A tremendous fire and fright afflicted my soul and at that moment, with a strength that was not my own, I seized the man standing at my right, pushed him to the left and quickly leaped into his place. No one observed me and the fever within was relieved. I was saved.

Now, at last, I looked at the man standing to the left whom, by my one act, I had deprived of life.

It was Vaněk.

He stood calmly, good-humoredly, suspecting nothing, and holding in his work-calloused, bruised hands a gun. He was looking straight ahead with the same frank gaze which I had always known him to have, and with the trustfulness of an honest countryman he awaited a just decision. Even a slight, though very touching, smile played on his lips and in his eyes reposed a cheerful friendliness for all things on earth.

EVERY FIFTH MAN

An unspeakable sorrow gripped me of a sudden. I wished to quickly dodge back to my former place, but the Captain caught sight of me.

"Stay in your place!" he roared, and turned ruddy to his forehead. His large eyes bulged out noticeably. "Whoever moves will be shot on the spot!"

All became silent. My heart seemed to pound furiously within me, but only at intervals. I looked around at Vaněk. He was smiling as he gazed out on the plain lying before us, over which the Colonel with some officers came riding towards us. Behind them advanced a company of some infantry regiment unfamiliar to me. All this happened quickly, rigorously, silently and withal mysteriously and ominously. My eyes roved from place to place while I waited an opportune moment to draw back Vaněk to his former place. But I dared not move again. The Captain watched me constantly.

Just then Lieutenant Schuster stepped up to our line and, seeming somehow taller and more dignified, counted out in his high-pitched voice, "One, two, three, four, five!" And seizing the soldier indicated by the number "five" by the collar he pulled him out in front of the line.

"One, two, three, four, five!" Vaněk was now drawn out in front. In embarrassment he smiled and looked about him good-naturedly as if he thought that he was to be elevated in rank or to be honored in some manner. He did not yet grasp what was really happening. But deep and genuine compassion, full of grief and pain, stifled me.

Schuster's high-pitched voice continued to sound, moving farther towards the left. In front of us stood several soldiers. They did not know what position to assume, confusedly looking about at the officers who stood dispersed over the field.

Increasing anguish held my heart and throat in a vise. All of us were pale and terror stricken. Vaněk was looking about and, like a little child, he turned and smiled at us. Whenever he felt that he was observed by one of the officers he straightened up and, according to military rule, gazed intently ahead into vacancy.

I recalled many moments spent with him and to my mind came the rending consciousness that Vaněk had three children at home.

"This is terrible," I whispered, quivering in every nerve. But I did not have the power to undertake a deed that would save his life. A sort of weakness of which I had not been conscious before, and which was due directly to the impotence of human nature, held me back. In my eyes a slight wave of heat, then tears and powerless rage followed each other in quick succession. I was crushed, but I could look at all that was happening about me somewhat more resolutely.

Schuster had finished counting.

Twenty-one men stood in the foreground.

The company which had just arrived with rapid step

and in unusual order sent out eight men who took from the selected men their weapons.

Vaněk became pale and his tall body from sheer weakness took on a crooked appearance.

"Dear God!" he moaned softly, and his bony, bruised hands were clasped. He looked around at me and I hung my head. A portion of some sort of prayer I remembered from childhood came to my tongue. I wanted to whisper "Forgive" to him, but even this word remained on my lips, for the order was given to fall in. Immediately Schuster, with unusual decision and haste, constantly admonishing someone in his high voice, which sounded strangely in my ears, led us away to the front ranks behind the retreating enemy infantry.

We pressed on like animals, obediently, rapidly and in utter speechlessness. We had all succumbed to the terrible result of the unjust punishment, and all of us were doubtless thinking of those who remained behind. My whole body trembled. Through my thoughts flashed all the incidents and all the figures of the soldiers, and longest to remain in my mind's eye was always Vaněk with his good-hearted, childlike smile. A great tenseness began gradually to overpower me, a hot wave rolled into my cheeks, and my ears in strained attention searched the varying hum for the sound of firing.

At that instant the collective discharge of many guns howled behind us. I cried out faintly. For a moment all became black before my eyes. In my breast something ached as if my heart had been torn out by force. My whole being was crushed under a weight of grief.

And I began to pray the Lord's Prayer fervently and sincerely as I had not been able to do since my earliest childhood.

JOSEPH SVATOPLUK MACHAR

(Born February 29, 1864, in Kolin.)

MACHAR spent his youth in Brandýs on the Elbe, which calm and lovely country he often describes in his poems and stories. After completing his course at the gymnasium in Prague and fulfilling his required military service he became, in 1891, a bank official in Vienna, where he lived until the outbreak of the world war, during the early period of which he was imprisoned on information furnished by the Austrian spy system, which asserted that a revolutionary, anti-Austrian poem of Machar's had been published in a Czech paper in the United States. The exigencies to which the spy system was put to trump up a case was well shown in the Machar affair, for the poem was indeed published in the United States, but it had previously appeared many times in Bohemia without giving offense to the Hapsburg government. In the newly organized Czechoslovak Republic, Machar has just been appointed General-Inspector of the Czechoslovak Army.

Machar's proximity to the Austrian capital and his distance from Prague gave him at once an insight into the clouded whirlpool of the empire's politics and a perspective on the life of his own countrymen, which a mere Viennese or a Praguer, respectively, could not attain. This insight he displays in his fearless attacks on subterfuge and hypocrisy on the one hand and flag-waving and drum-beating patriotism on the other.

It is chiefly as a poet that Machar is known. He uses the medium of verse to fling his challenge to wordy, but deedless, idealism among his compatriots, to proclaim rebellion against empty religion, the fruitless promises of politicians, the inanity of a so-called social system forever degrading the Magdalens and letting weeds spring up where roses should bloom. He always places himself on the side of the oppressed or downtrodden, even though he many times invited and received a storm of violent abuse by refusing to idealize the sordid and insisting that squalor and meanness were foul, though just as true as the beautiful. Eminently a realist of the Neruda type, he has had to fight for the recognition of his principles, as well as of himself, as their promulgator.

Machar's best-known poetical works are "V Záři Hellenského Slunce" (In the Glow of a Hellenic Sun), advocating a return to the robust faith of the Greeks; "Confiteor," full of scepticism and heartaches; "Bez Názvu (Without a Name), an aggressive attack on life's hard conditions; "Zde by Měly Kvésti Růže" (Here Roses Should Bloom), depicting the depth of sorrows of womankind; "Magdalen," a romance in blank verse, translated into eight languages, detailing the story of a woman who has once fallen and whom relentless fate, in the form of the self-appointed censors of society, pursues to the end of a career that might have been beautiful; "Tristium Vindobona," a mirror of Czech national psychology; "Golgotha," a discussion of the Roman Empire; "Jed z Judey" (Poison from Judea), thoughts suggested by monuments of ancient culture.

Machar's prose, like his poetry, represents the changing attitude of mind towards all big, vital questions. His reflections on life are presented in the many sketches in "Stará Prosa" (Old Prose Tales); "Hrst Belletrie" (A Handful of Tales); Stories in Prose (1901–1903) and two later collections with the same titles; "Krajiny, Lidé a Netopýři" (Lands, People and Bats); "Veršem i Prosou" (In Verse and Prose); "Kniha Feuilletonů" (A Book of Feuilletons); "Řím" (Rome), a discussion of ancient, papal and modern Rome; "Konfesse Literáta" (The Confessions of a Literary Man), a diary of a man striving to express his life in terms of literary service.

The story used here is from his "**Stará Prosa**" and is done in his characteristic manner.

THEORIES OF HEROISM

BY JOSEPH SVATOPLUK MACHAR

"It's ten years since then," the Captain resumed, after long urging. "Our battalion was in Hercegovina. The devil was to blame for that campaign. You have no doubt read in the papers enough about all the trials, misfortunes and sufferings endured. Bah! that's all only a shadow of the horrible reality. That was not war—it was a chase after a rabble of wild men in which the necks of the pursuers were in danger every second, and if I were to tell all that we suffered you would say, 'It isn't possible for a man to live through all that.' And yet a man had to live through it. Habit— A man gets used to everything in this world.

"But to get to what I really want to tell I will leave out the description of all the skirmishes and battles which we engaged in that fall and winter. I will pass over at once to Gacko.

"We struck Gacko in March. There our company remained in garrison. At that time I was a First Lieutenant.

"Gacko is an abominable nest. A dirty, frowning village of Christians and Turks who would gladly have killed us in perfect unanimity of mind. Whether a a youth or an old man met you—each one fairly pierced you with his eyes.

"The women there were very odd. You hear often of the beauty of Hercegovinian women, you see their pictures—I ought not to spoil your illusions. I looked at every woman that I met, and I arrived at an opposite conclusion on the beauty question. All of them were ugly, positively hideous and withered, as if they had never been young. If there happened to be one here and there that was really young she was ugly just like the rest.

"The Turkish women were just the same. We saw them often. They were veiled up to their eyes—but those eyes sufficed for the observer. They were eyes, altogether so stupid, so entirely without shine or beauty that they gave birth among us to the permanent joke that their faces were veiled out of consideration for our refined sense of beauty. And, strangely enough, too, this joke was taken up and soon spread over all Hercegovina.

"And the life there! Drill, sentinel inspection, drill and sentinel inspection! It was a dog's life—worse than the marches and battles which we had to go through before. Our only joy, in reality, our only consolation was wine. And a man sat in the casino (it was a filthy hut, one large room with a low, smoked-up ceiling) and drank and forgot. Yes, a man forgot and drank—and frequently drank down his whole future.

THEORIES OF HEROISM

"The entertainment there was not startlingly varied. We played cards, talked, sang. We liked to strike up the melancholy Hercegovinian songs. Our conversations were about every possible thing on earth. Often we waded into subjects which none of us understood.

"One evening I returned with my division from a sentry inspection. We were tired to death. For ten whole hours we had climbed cliffs, crawled through ravines and waded through snow up to our knees. The wind blew first from one direction and then from the other and dashed frosty pieces of snow into our faces. The men did not even eat or undress, but crawled into their beds and slept.

"I entered the barracks and sank into a chair. Wine and cigarettes revived me to some extent.

"In the casino it was lively.

"My comrades sat or stood around a table near the stove. They were all absorbed apparently in an interesting conversation. At first I did not understand a word, for several of them were talking at once. The discussion evidently had become intensely interesting, now only one question with its respective answer at a time was to be heard, the rest listening intently.

"I shoved my chair a little closer.

"'And I insist on my own view,' said Lieutenant Martini, with animation, 'and I repeat once more that a man who values his life at nothing, who has nothing to lose in life, is the bravest soldier.'

"Martini was an Italian. He was tall with sunburnt cheeks, raven hair and moustache, eyes dark as coals and a quick temper. When he talked he gesticulated with his hands and shouted as if he stood before a division of his soldiers.

"'And I dispute that,' after a pause, spoke Lieutenant Šetina, a Czech from Bohemia. 'A soldier to whom life is nothing cannot value it and will risk it for every piece of foolishness, on every trivial occasion—that's poor principle. Such a man is not a hero in my eyes. A hero must know the value of his life. He protects it as his dearest possession as long, of course, as his defense of it squares with his military honor and conscience. He must know that with his life there disappears a sword from the ranks of the army of his country and therefore he ought to appreciate the worth of his life.'

"'Šetina is right,' interrupted Captain Kristovic, a native of Croatia, rocking on his chair.

"'I still insist on my own view,' burst out Martini. 'One sword more or less—his Majesty always has a substitute. No one but a philistine or a coward would act as Šetina says. An Austrian officer sees no heroism in it.'

"Šetina's cheeks flamed. He struck the table with his clenched fist and cried out, 'And I again see in your ideal of heroism only an example of folly! It is wholly unreasonable! Just call back to mind the history of the wars of 1859 and 1866. The Austrian officers con-

THEORIES OF HEROISM

sidered it dishonorable to lie down on the ground or to kneel behind their firing-lines. And the consequence? The officers were shot down at the very first charge! That is a slightly illusory heroism. I shall risk my life only on an important occasion—in matters of nonsense I shall protect it. Thus every respectable soldier feels and does—unless he is a crack-brained lunatic!'

"'That's true!'

"'Šetina is right.'

"'Wholly right.'

"A few other expressions of approval were heard around the room.

"Martini's hand trembled. His dark face grew crimson. Ominous lightnings flashed from his eyes.

"'Lieutenant,' he said, controlling himself and forcing his voice into the tones of a formal conversation, 'I demand that you moderate your expressions. That is the opinion I hold.'

"He laid special stress on the word 'I.' We understood him. Martini was known to be the best swordsman in the whole battalion. Neither did his revolver ever miss aim.

"Suddenly we began to comprehend the gravity of the situation. However, before a single appeasing word could be spoken, Šetina arose and said with forced calmness, 'Lieutenant, I have given my private judgment of a man who would, according to your principles, lay claim to the name of a hero.'

"A smothered assent was heard around the room. We felt that Šetina was acting with dignity.

"This approbation fired Martini even more.

"'Lieutenant, I remind you once more that behind that idea I stand,' burst out Šetina, likewise angered.

"'Take that back,' roared Martini.

"'I'm not afraid of you,' answered Šetina, and looked icily into his eyes.

"We all arose. Šetina was the favorite of all the officers of the battalion. His complexion was as fair as a girl's. He had blue eyes and a blond moustache. In the service he was without a flaw. As a companion he was always pleasant and ever a perfect friend. Here in Prague he had an aged mother and a sweetheart. He was only waiting for the end of the campaign, when he was to be made a first lieutenant, and then he intended to marry. He always wrote to his mother once a week and to his sweetheart every other day. This letter he always wrote regularly, even if it were only a few lines in length. Sometimes there was something impressively funny about it. I had often seen him writing on the very battle-field. He would sit in the snow warming his rigid right hand on a cigarette, and would write on a piece of paper held on his knee.

"Martini wasn't much liked among us. He was a cynic, feared for his dexterity at fencing and for his sure aim with the revolver. He liked to mock, with special malevolence, at every sacred feeling known to man. He himself had not an atom of sentiment. Of his parents or home he never spoke a word. His soldiers he treated roughly and without a touch of feeling. He had never liked Šetina, probably because of the popularity the latter enjoyed, due to the charm of his personality.

"Šetina could not retract his words—that was certain; he could not lower his dignity to that extent. We tried to appease Martini, we explained to him in the mildest manner—in vain.

"'Take back—take back everything,' he raged.

"Šetina stood there pale and spoke no word. It was as if a horrible foreboding had taken possession of his soul. At intervals his fingers dug into his palms spasmodically, and his lips quivered.

"We pleaded with Martini. He only sneered maliciously.

"Here and there a few threats were heard.

"Martini tossed his head, looked around the casino and said, bitingly: 'Gentlemen, has any one else anything against me? Just be kind enough to come forward. We'll settle it all at once.'

"A duel was unavoidable.

"I went out with Šetina into the dark night. To the hut where he lived it was only a few hundred feet.

"The sky was overclouded. The snow cast into this darkness a sort of grayish obscurity.

"Šetina did not speak. He was whistling indistinctly some sort of march in quick tempo. We reached his house. He extended his hand to me.

"'I'd invite you in for a glass of cognac—but forgive me this time—I must write to my dear one,' he said with a sort of forced quietness. 'Apropos—tomorrow you'll assist me, will you not?' And pressing my hand he disappeared.

"Early in the morning of the next day we quickly went through the formalities of a duel. After long talking, explaining, pleading and threatening, the Lieutenant-Colonel gave his permission—that's true—but on the whole it was, after all, only an underhand sort of affair, this forced duel. There was not enough powerful argument to satisfy a higher court, and yet the affair could not be settled otherwise than by the use of the revolver. You see, Šetina could not easily manage a sword. His right hand was somewhat crippled from a ball which had struck him during our march over the Hercegovinian rocks. By the way, I recall how he often bit his lips until they bled whenever there was changeable weather. That's how much the wound burned and stung.

"The casino was chosen as the scene of action. It couldn't take place elsewhere—the circumstance, the unsettled condition of things, and all that. I was Šetina's second.

"Two army revolvers were brought.

"With a trembling hand I loaded them. I had an evil foreboding.

"The tables and chairs were shoved into one corner. The casino throughout its length was cleared. From

THEORIES OF HEROISM 131

wall to wall, lengthwise of the room, it was eighteen paces. We measured fifteen paces and marked the distance with chalk.

"The battle for life and death was to begin.

"I looked at Šetina. I scrutinized his features carefully for a sign of fear, anxiety or some sort of misgiving. I am to some extent superstitious, and I would have foretold a bad ending. I saw nothing. He calmly placed himself in position and smiled blissfully, as if thoughts of his bride and of his mother were occupying him. At intervals he snapped the fingers of his left hand.

"I took new hope. Šetina was also a good shot—at that moment he was calm—what then could happen? Involuntarily I smiled at my former anxieties.

"At the signal 'three' the rivals were to fire simultaneously.

"My last attempt at a reconciliation was rejected by both—by Martini wrathfully, by Šetina with a smile.

"The order sounded. Two flashes sped across the space of the room, which immediately filled with smoke. We heard a heavy fall and the clink of breaking glass.

"With arms outstretched Šetina lay near the wall with his face to the ground. His forehead was shattered. Portions of the brain were on the wall. From his head the blood was spurting. He was dead.

"His ball struck several feet above Martini's head into a portrait of the emperor and broke the glass.

"Heaven only knows how he aimed. I suspect that he purposely aimed high.

"That is the end of the story. I think of it very often. But what is the use of it all, now? Oftentimes those two theories of heroism float through my head, and it seems to me that that combat was a duel of theories. Šetina's theory fell. Šetina himself gave the greatest argument in proof of Martini's theory. He died for a piece of folly, but he died like a hero. I constantly see him before me. Oh, that life was indeed worthy of a more beautiful end."

"And Martini?" I asked the Captain, much affected.

"Martini?" he repeated as he spat disgustedly. "Martini is today the owner of a large estate. He married a rich girl whom he did not love and withdrew from the army.

"And you poets," he said, bitterly, after a pause, "find everywhere and depict always 'poetic justice'! Look for it in real life! Find it—if you can! To be sure, poetry is only a pastime for wealthy people— and such must not have their nerves shaken by some harsh truth. You have everything smoothed out— everything lovely—it all fairly sparkles—scoundrels are punished and virtuous lovers secure each other— but in reality—

"But lest I forget—Šetina's mother was stricken with paralysis on hearing of her son's death. What became of his sweetheart I don't know. She has probably become someone's wife."

BOŽENA VÍKOVÁ-KUNĚTICKÁ

(Born 1863 in Pardubice.)

BOZENA VIKOVA, the wife of J. Vik, an official in one of the large sugar factories of Czechoslovakia, adopted as a pen-name "Kunětická," after the place where she spent her childhood.

The discrimination practised against womankind in the social and economic world forms the basic idea of many of her stories and novels. Her introduction to literature was, however, in sketches of the less vital but fully as painful, sordid, little tragedies of a woman's life of which "Spiritless," which follows, is an example. Mrs. Víková-Kunětická has eight collections of short stories to her credit and six longer romances—"Vdova po Chirurgovi" (The Surgeon's Widow), "Minulost" (The Past); and "Justýna Holdanova" and "Medřická," named for their chief characters; "Vzpoura" (Revolt) and "Pán" (The Master).

She stands as the champion of women for the preservation of their individuality against total submersion in the being of their husbands and she is often accused of extreme feminism. She never relinquishes for a moment her demand for equal personal purity in the parties to a marriage contract.

As a playwright her comedies, "Sběratelka Starožitností" (The Collector of Curiosities), "Cop" (The Braid), "Neznámá Pevnina" (Unknown Territory) and "Přítěž" (Ballast), won favor and are frequently produced. Her dramas, "V Jařmu" (In the Yoke), "Holčička" (The Little Girl) and "V Bludišti" (In a Maze), are less successful as dramas than as feminist propaganda.

Mrs. Víková-Kunětická was honored by her countrymen by election to the Bohemian Parliament some ten years ago. The Austrian government with its customary indifference to all progressive ideas, under one pretext or another refused her permission to take her seat in the assembly. Her election at that time was the first example in central Europe of similar recognition for a woman. In the present congress of the Czechoslovak Republic there are twelve women representatives.

SPIRITLESS

BY BOŽENA VÍKOVA-KUNĚTICKÁ

THE first cold breeze of winter blew over the country and swept from a tree the first faded leaf. Could it indeed be true that the leaves had begun to wither so early? Yes, truly, for look! the leaf is sere and trembling and almost spasmodically curled up as if it had expired in the very act of its struggle with death. And now it flutters downward through the branches of the tree which is crowned with such an abundance of green foliage that it seems as if a cloud had settled on it or a mournful pall of the future which gave no promise of spring blossoms, songs of birds or whispers of lovers. The sad little leaf had indeed fallen in the midst of all the greenness spread underneath the blue heavens and lay upon the grass where the first dying blade shivered and sighed among its mates!

"Alas! The leaves are fading!" cried a sweet young wife as she closed the window which she had opened a few moments previously in order that the fresh breath of morn might enter the sleeping-room.

She had opened it thus after the departure of her husband every morning for the last four months and, filled with delightful intoxication, she had presented herself to the rays of the sun, sighing in the very excess of her bliss.

Today the chill breath of the wind rudely touched her hand and brow for the first time and caused her to experience a disagreeable sensation of disappointment, aye, of sorrow.

The young wife turned away from the window with a sense of weariness which she herself scarcely comprehended. She cast her eyes over the room which was still in disorder and filled with the breath of sleep. The air was heavy and the silence of the apartment productive of melancholy and gloom. She stepped to the mirror to begin her toilet and discovered that her eyes were tired-looking, without their usual luster, her lips were dry and compressed, the pink was gone from her cheeks and her hands were colorless, cold and strangely weak and limp.

She meditated, thinking what kind of a ribbon to put into her hair. Long she pondered on what gown to wear and her thoughts finally reverted to the subject of what to cook for dinner.

She had reflected thus each day for the past four months, at first in a sort of enchanted spell, later with something akin to impatience and now as if from habit or a sense of duty. On the table still stood the cups out of which she and her husband had been drinking coffee, before he departed for his office. They had not conversed much either today or yesterday and had breakfasted with some degree of constraint, for they were intent on the *necessity* of eating, which fact had not been before apparent to them because—well, because—they had been in love.

But now for a number of days both had sipped their coffee to the last drop and afterwards carefully wiped their lips as if feeling the need of some occupation. The husband had arisen, taken his hat, cane and some documents (the young wife noticed that he always took some sort of papers) and, kissing her on the lips, he departed for his office, while she had called after him with a bright voice: "Bring me something in your pocket, Otto! Don't forget! Perhaps you'll see some of my favorite apples—some 'Míšenská' somewhere and you'll bring them."

He had answered briefly from the hallway, because he was in a hurry, "Why can't you send Veronica?" (Veronica was the maid.)

"But I want the apples from you, dear Otto," the young wife had cried after him sadly.

"I have many cares on my mind today," he had replied.

"What are they?"

"Oh, you don't understand such things."

"But you will bring my apple? Do you **hear**? Don't forget!"

Her last words reached her husband as his hand touched the knob of the house door and he did not reply to them because he did not wish to cause an unnecessary noise in the house.

At noon he indeed brought his wife two, three or four of her favorite "Míšenská" apples and, laying them on the table, he asked at once for his dinner that he might again depart as soon as possible.

They both felt ennui stealing on them. Heaven knows why they were tired. They slept soundly without dreams. Often when alone together they were silent and each was at a loss for a topic for conversation. The young wife with the instinct born in every woman divined that the touch of her hands no longer aroused a thrill in her husband's senses and that he kissed her without any tremors of pleasure, but rather in a hasty, careless, perfunctory manner. And she herself felt exhausted, languishing, discontented and saw no fixed purpose anywhere.

What was the matter?

She discovered as she gazed into the mirror that blue was unbecoming to her and, looking down at her hands, she saw that she had not trimmed her nails for some days. That was the only thing to which she could devote her attention, as everything in her household was bright, shining and new—every article was in its appointed place. The perfect order and exactness of it all was enough to drive one mad.

It entered her mind that it might be a good plan to cook lentils today for dinner. She wanted a new fragrance in her kitchen—an odor to which it heretofore was unaccustomed, as she had not yet cooked lentils during her married life.

SPIRITLESS

She continued to look at herself in the glass stupidly and without interest. She had a beautifully molded figure, but her inspection of self did not impress her pleasurably or otherwise, because her goal was attained—her purpose achieved. She possessed charming lips and large, clear eyes which she opened wide, as if in constant wonder. On her left hand shone the golden wedding-ring which proclaimed her a wife and which proved in her eyes that the object of her life was accomplished. She was married! Ah, well, at any rate she had no more worries about a husband such as she had at first heard expressed by her sisters when they had finished school and which she herself had felt when she donned her first long dress and realized that the most important period of her life had arrived.

What a bore it had been at that time! To be compelled to wear a constant smile, encouraging and yet modest, to drop the eyes shyly, to bow her head, to meditate on what she should say in order to preserve the proprieties of what is allowable and what is not; to devote constant attention to every step, to every "Oh!" "Ah!" "Indeed!" "Certainly," "Perhaps," "Oh yes!" "By no means!" and all the expressions for which she would be held to account before the entire company and by which she proved her good breeding, knowledge, modesty and dignity in gracing her home in the future. How many times she had repeated, as she walked lightly by her partner's side through the dancing-hall which was warm to suffocation, "What an atmosphere! Does it not appear to you, sir, that the atmosphere is heavy?" Or else at picnics or outings while the sound of music filled the air and all around were cheerful and gay, she conventionally uttered her admiration thus: "How beautiful all this is! I love music, and especially do I love to listen to the notes of a flute!" And all the time she was studying the words she would be called upon to utter next, in order that they should be both proper and agreeable. She would bow, extend the fingers of her hand in greeting, sit very severely upright in her chair and thank in a very cold manner all gentlemen who were of an uncertain or unprofessional occupation, as her code did not admit those without means to her favored circle.

Ah, well! The golden band shines on her finger now, and with it all the past is banished, the present solved and the future ordained.

"Well, then, lentils it shall be today." Lentils are certainly not rare, but they will cause a change in the entire atmosphere of her clean, shiny household. As soon as he reaches the steps her husband will be met with the fragrance from the kitchen and will know that she is cooking lentils for his dinner.

At the thought of her husband she felt a tiny wave of trouble in her soul. It seemed to her that she ought to have something new to say to him, something kind and affable, but she explained this desire as a consequence of the habit she had been trained in of always making an effort to be pleasant to him.

SPIRITLESS 141

She interpreted it all in her own charming little head as singular that she should allow herself any critical or censuring reflections which marriage itself abolishes and excludes.

Was not everything in her matrimonial existence just as proper as her whole life and its well-ordered details had always been?

Her first kiss given and accepted after a formal engagement, her tears at the altar which were in accordance with strict etiquette, her toilettes, her education which she had received in a convent and which she had concluded with the reading of a few books of which it was perfectly proper to speak in polite society —all these had certainly been eminently proper. What more could she wish, what more could her husband demand?

Some day she would become a mother, and then of course all would be changed. She would have enough to relate to her husband then—the child would laugh and cry and make its first little attempts, and later it would learn to walk, to pray, then would attend school and, in the vista of the future, she even beheld its marriage.

All these things would occur in the same succession as they had occurred to her ancestors; it had not been different with her great-grandmother, her grandmother nor even with her mother. Her mother, to be sure, had never felt any uneasiness regarding her husband and how to interest him. Her father was an honest merchant in linen goods and her mother helped him make sales in the shop. No time remained for her to have similar reflections, and her conversations with her husband always appeared important and intensely interesting to both. Their business brought them a tidy income and assured their daughters a handsome dowry.

Ah! How well she remembered the little shop under the arcade into which the daughters were never allowed to enter lest there might appear to be a connection between the shop and their sweet little faces which were only partially hidden by the rich veils. *They* were not meant to be salesgirls, for they were destined to be young ladies of the most cultured and most select circles of society.

* * * * * * *

The young wife laid aside the blue ribbon and fastened on a pink one instead. She discovered that it really was much more becoming to her, and as a result she felt a corresponding degree of satisfaction.

She walked out of the bedroom, gave her hand to the angular maid to be kissed and passed on through the remaining rooms in which the best of order prevailed.

There really was *nothing* to think of!

She remembered again that her husband would soon arrive and once more experienced a disquieting uneasiness. What would they talk about today at dinner? Perhaps he does not like lentils and will be vexed when Veronica brings the dish on the table. Perhaps, how-

SPIRITLESS 143

ever, he may like them and then he will be gay. After all, what of it? They *must* talk of something! Maybe one of the apples will be decayed and she will show him the worm and cry, "Oh! oh! oh! dear Otto, a worm! Such a big, long worm!" and he of course will step on it and thus conversation will ensue.

* * * * * * *

Alas! the apple was not wormy and her husband did not indeed like lentils, and during dinner he was somewhat morose, at any rate dull and lazy in thought and act.

He cleaned his teeth for a long time with a toothpick which she herself had fashioned for him by winding strings of small beads around a tapering quill, according to a pattern she had seen at the convent.

She recalled that this morning she had seen the first faded leaf fall from a tree. "Just think, Otto, the leaves have begun to fall," she said, gazing at him with her large, clear eyes which hid nothing from those returning her gaze.

"Well, that's excellent!" cried her husband.

"Why 'excellent,' Otto dear?"

"Because the falling of the leaves ushers in the season when, as before, I shall go among my old friends to spend the long winter evenings."

"Where is it you will go 'among friends'?"

"Oh, down to the inn for a space of two short hours. You have nothing against it, have you, love?"

His young wife reflected whether or not it was

proper for her husband to do what he had just proposed. She reflected that the husband of one of her friends and other men she knew of often went "among friends" to talk over things of which their wives had never heard in the convents in which they had been brought up.

Her mind was considerably pacified by this reflection, and so she answered with a smile, "Why, no, Otto, dear; I have nothing against it! Why, just think, what *could we* find to talk about together all those long evenings to come?"

And that day when the first yellow leaf fell from the tree, crowned with so much greenness—for the first time, but not the last—the young wife sat at home—alone.

BOŽENA NĚMCOVÁ

(Born February 5, 1820, in Vienna; died January 20, 1862, in Prague.)

THE first of the realistic writers of Bohemia was Božena Němcová, who stands unqualifiedly foremost among the women authors of her nation. Němcová spent her childhood in the foothill region of Ratibořice on the Silesian border, where is laid the scene of her best-known and most-loved novel of country life, "Babička" (The Grandmother), which has gone into dozens of editions and has been translated into many different languages. Frances Gregor, author of "The Story of Bohemia," made the English translation of this beautiful story, which Němcová admitted was a picture of her own life and that of her brothers and sisters under the sheltering love of one of the dearest and most typical characters in Czech literature—"the grandmother." Not a trace of bitterness appears in the entire novel, though it was written when Němcová was experiencing nothing but hardship and sorrow in a most unhappy married life, and after death had removed her chief joy—her eldest son, Hynek. A bride at seventeen, Němcová, whose maiden name was

Barbora Panklova, cultivated her genius, which had already shown itself, under the guidance of literary men with whom she came in contact in Prague, where her husband, an official in the Austrian government service, was stationed for a while. Through her husband's necessarily frequent removals she became well acquainted with various parts of Bohemia and also made five extended sojourns in Slovensko (Slovakia), where she studied the people and collected the customs, traditions, tales and folk lore in general which she later used untouched in her collections of fairy tales and legends, or wove into short stories and novels whose characters and plots were her own creation. Then, too, her intimate knowledge of the people among whom she lived and sought her friends aided materially in giving her a true insight into their souls as well as a thorough knowledge of the dialects predominating in each section which she later took as the background for her stories.

Němcová's initial literary efforts (1844–1848) were made in the field of lyric poetry which expressed a deeply patriotic feeling. She felt that women should participate in the nationalistic struggles of the Czechs who were emerging from two centuries of the tomb after their crushing defeat at the Battle of White Mountain in 1620. All her later writings likewise breathe her Slavonic sympathies.

Very soon after her poems began to appear she was urged by Karel Jaromir Erben, one of the foremost folklorists of the day, to put into literary form the great wealth of fairy tales, fables, legends and other lore she had been gathering. Her response was the splendid collection entitled "National Fairy Tales and Legends" which was soon followed by her "Slovak Fairy Tales and Legends." Her discussions and descriptions of the customs and manners of the groups she learned to know throughout Bohemia and North Hungary—chiefly in the Slovak districts—are of real ethnographical value.

Němcová's first novels, "Obrázek Vesnický" (A Village Picture), "Dlouhá Noc" (The Long Night) and "Domácí Nemoc" (Home Sickness), belong to the same period (1846–1847), when she was but twenty-six. Her next novelettes, "Baruška" (Barbara) and "Sestry" (The Sisters), touch on social questions for which she suggests, unobtrusively, to be sure, a solution. A most ingenious plot with a pleasing and unusual romance characterizes her novel, "Karla" (Carla). In the same year, 1855, she wrote and published her masterpiece, "Babička." In rapid succession came "Divá Bára" (Bewitched Bára); "Chýže Pod Horami" (The Cottage on the Mountainside), depicting the beautiful customs and fresh, unspoiled character of the Slovak mountaineers; "Pohorská Vesnice" (The Mountain Village), a story of the Bohemian Forest region; "Dobrý Člověk" (The Good Man); "Chudí Lidé" (Poor People) and "V Zámku a Podzámčí" (In the Castle and Below), which presents the eternal conflict of wealth and poverty, high estate and low, and is a direct indictment of society.

The invigorating wholesomeness of Němcová's stories agreeably penetrates the consciousness of the reader, who is refreshed and inspired by their simple nobility without feeling that he has been "preached at." Němcová's method is marked by a simplicity, untrammeled directness, and a conviction of truth, which enlist one's interest immediately. The traditional "happy ending" which the American craves and insists on in most of his novels and plays has the nearest Slav counterpart in Němcová's thorough optimism, her absolute refusal to be cynical or bitter. Somehow, despite the inevitable sorrows which the truth of life forces her to depict, she leads her characters from "the slough of despond" to a logical "consummation devoutly to be wished." This trait is the more remarkable in view of the fact that all the romance and joy was crushed out of her own life, which became a daily sordid struggle for bread for her family and herself, especially after the death of her son and the loss by her husband, who was never sympathetic with her ideals, of his position under the government. Němcová has created many faithfully drawn Czech and Slovak characters, her women especially being typical of their nation. She writes with a vigor, picturesqueness and purity, combined with the characteristic quiet Slav humor and poetic idealism, which never fail to appeal.

While "Bewitched Bára" is one of her earlier stories, it nevertheless represents her manner and her choice of material. Superstition is now by no means generally characteristic of the Czechs and Slovaks, but at the time Němcová wrote her story, about sixty-five years ago, rationalistic teachings were not as widely disseminated as now. This story had the effect of weaning the people from much ignorant credulity and beliefs in omens, signs and the power of so-called supernatural beings.

Němcová has evolved a character at once strong, beautiful and independent in the person of the dauntless Bára who through her own investigations—she was practically self-trained—had freed herself from all the superstitious fears which enchained the souls of nearly all the others in the village. Then, too, Němcová clearly shows here the value in education of nature and natural methods, a subject she introduces, together with other social reform tendencies, in her "Pohorská Vesnice" (The Mountain Village), which she regarded as her best work, placing it above her "Babička," which has been far more widely loved. The friendship of the two girls, Bára and Elška, whose social advantages were so widely different, is a wholesome, happy picture. For the sake of her devotion for Elška, Bára carries out the traditional custom of young girls in Bohemia who seek to know whence their lover will come, by casting wreaths of flowers into a stream before sunrise of the Day of St. John the

Baptist. She herself does not believe in the custom, but weaves and throws her wreath to please Elška, who in the secure refuge of Bára's affection confides her deepest feeling to the one understanding soul.

"BEWITCHED BÁRA"

BY BOŽENA NĚMCOVÁ

I

VESTEC is a large village and has a church and school also. Near the church is the parsonage; beside it the sexton's house. The mayor also lives in the center of the community. On the very edge of the hamlet stands the little cottage of the village herdsman. Beyond the cottage extends a long valley surmounted on both sides by hills grown over mainly with pines. Here and there is a clearing or green meadow with sparsely growing white-barked, bright-leaved birches, those maidens of the tree world which nature had permitted to grow there to cheer up the dismal pines and firs and the somber oaks and beeches. In the middle of the valley among the meadows and fields flowed a river directly past the herdsman's cottage. On its banks at this point grew an alder and a willow.

The village herdsman was called Jacob and lived with his daughter, Bára, in the last cottage. Jacob was in his sixties and Bára was his first-born and only child. To be sure he had wished for a son to inherit his name, but when Bára grew older he did not regret that she was a girl. She was dearer to him than a son and many times he thought to himself: "Even though she is a girl, she is my own. I shall die like a man and I have, as a father, a stepping-stone to heaven."

Jacob was born in the village. Being an orphan, he had to go into service from childhood. He served as goose-herder, drover, cowherd, neat-herder, as hostler and ploughman until he reached the highest degree of the rank, becoming the community herdsman. That offered a good living and he could now marry.

He was given a cottage to live in to his death. The peasants brought him wood to his very courtyard. He could keep a cow. Bread, butter, eggs, milk, vegetables, of all these he received supplies each week. Each year, linen enough for three shirts and for two pairs of drawers was supplied to him, and, in addition, two pair of shoes, corduroys, a jacket, a broad-brimmed hat, and every other year a fur coat and a heavy blanket. Besides that on each holy day and church feast day he received pastry and his wages, so that even at the parsonage they did not fare better.

In short it was a good position and Jacob, though he was lacking in good looks, uncommunicative and morose, could nevertheless have gotten a wife, but he was in no hurry. In the summer he made the excuse that he had no time to look around among the girls because it was pasturing season. In the winter he was busy carving out wooden shoes, and in the evenings when the lads sought out the society of their girl friends he preferred to sit a while at the inn. When

"BEWITCHED BÁRA" 153

it happened that a wife would come to the inn for her husband, Jacob always congratulated himself that there was no one to come looking for him. It never bothered him that they poked fun at him, saying he'd be an old bachelor and that old bachelors must, after death, stay in purgatory and tie sand into bundles. Thus passed his fortieth year. Then someone told him that should he die childless he could not get to heaven, that children are steps up to heaven. Somehow that worked itself into Jacob's brain and when the thought had thoroughly matured he went to the town mayor and married his maid, Bára.

Bára was a pretty girl in her youthful years. The boys liked to dance with her, and several of them used to go a-wooing her, but they were none of them the marrying sort. When Jacob asked her to become his wife she figured that she had three decades behind her, and though she was not particularly in love with Jacob she gave her promise to him, thinking to herself, "Better one's own sheaf than someone else's stack." So they were married and the mayor prepared a fine wedding for them.

A year later a girl child was born to them whom they named Bára after her mother. Jacob scratched his head a little when they told him it was a girl and not a boy, but the midwife consoled him by telling him she resembled him as closely as one egg resembles another.

Some days after the birth of the girl a mishap occurred in Jacob's home. A neighbor woman stopped in to see the convalescent and found her lying near the fireplace half dead. She gave the alarm, and the women came running hither, including the midwife, who resuscitated Bára. They learned from her that she was cooking her husband's dinner and, forgetting that a woman, after confinement, must never emerge from her room precisely at noon or after the Angelus, remained standing in the kitchen under the chimney and went on cooking. And then, she said, something rustled past her ears like an evil wind, spots floated before her eyes, something seemed to pull her by the hair and felled her to the floor.

"That was the noon-witch!" they all cried.

"Let us see if she has not exchanged a strange child for your Bára," one of them suggested and ran to the cradle. At once they all crowded around and took the baby from the cradle, unwrapped and examined it. One of them said: "It is a changeling, it is, surely! It has such big eyes!" Another cried, "She has a large head!" A third passed judgment on the child as having short legs, and each had something different to say. The mother was frightened, but the midwife after conscientiously examining the babe decided that it was Bára's very own child. Nevertheless, more than one of the old gossips continued to insist that the child was a changeling left there by the witch who appears at midday.

After that mishap Jacob's wife somehow never re-

"BEWITCHED BÁRA" 155

covered and in a few years after continual illness she died. Jacob remained alone with his little girl. Regardless of the fact that they urged him to marry again on account of the young child, he did not wish to do so. He watched over her as over a little lambkin, all alone, and well indeed he cared for her. When she grew up the schoolmaster sent word that Jacob should send her to school, and though Jacob regarded reading and writing as unnecessary, nevertheless he heeded. All winter Bára attended school, but in the spring when the pasturing began and also work in the field he could not get along without her. From springtime until fall the school, for the greater part of the week, was closed on a latch, the schoolmaster and the children also working in the fields, each according to his strength. The next winter Bára could not attend school any more, for she had to learn to spin and weave.

When Bára reached the age of fifteen not a girl in the entire village could equal her in strength and size. Her body was large-boned, of strong muscles, but of perfect symmetry. She was as agile as a trout. Her complexion was dark brown, in part naturally and in part due to the sun and wind, for, even in the heat of summer, never would she veil her face as did the village girls. Her head seemed to be large, but that was due to her mass of hair, black as a raven and long and coarse as horsehair. She had a low forehead, a short, blunt nose, a mouth that was rather large, with full lips, but healthy and as red as blood. Her teeth were strong and always glisteningly white. Her most beautiful feature was her eyes, and precisely on account of them she had to suffer much mockery from people. They nicknamed her, saying she had a "bull's eye." She did indeed have large eyes, unusually so and as blue as the cornflower, with long black lashes. Above her eyes arched thick black eyebrows.

When Bára frowned her face resembled the sky covered with black clouds, from which only a bit of blue shone forth. But she seldom wore a frown, except when the youngsters called her names, saying she had bull's eyes. Then her eyes flashed with anger and often she would burst into tears. But Jacob would always say: "You foolish girl, why do you mind them? I, too, have big eyes. And even if they are 'bull's eyes,' that's nothing bad. Why, the dumb animals can look at a man far more kindly than those human beings there!" At this he would always point with his stick towards the village. In later years, however, when she was stronger, none of the youngsters dared to hurt her, for she gave quick payment for every affront. Strong boys were unable to conquer her in a fight, for when mere strength failed her she used all sorts of manœuvers or helped herself by her nimbleness. In that way she won peace for herself.

Bára had so many unusual characteristics that it was not to be wondered at that the neighbors talked about her. Unable to interpret such a nature, the women began again to assert that she was, after all, a "change-

"BEWITCHED BÁRA" 157

ling," and if not, that the noon-witch had most undoubtedly taken her under her power. By this utterance all the actions of the girl were explained and excused, but as a consequence the villagers either avoided or feared her and only a few souls truly loved her. Whoever thought to anger her had only to say "Bewitched Bára!" But he who thought that this particular nickname offended her worse than any other was mistaken.

To be sure she had heard tales of noon-witches, evening specters, of the water-man, the fire-glow man who lives in the forest, and about the will-o'-the-wisps, the devil and ghosts. She had heard of all of these among the children, but she feared none of them. While she was still small her father used to take her out with him to the pasture and there she played the whole livelong day with her dog, Lišaj, who, next to her father, was her dearest playmate. Her father wasted few words on her, but sat and carved wooden shoes, raising his eyes at times to look at the herd, and if it were not all together, he would send Lišaj to return the cow or heifer, which the dog would always do, according to orders. When necessary, he himself would get up and make several circuits of the herd. When Bára was larger she accompanied Lišaj on his rounds, and if a cow tried to sniff at her, Lišaj would at once drive it away. As she grew older, in case of need she would often drive the herd out for her father. The cows knew her voice as well as Jacob's horn. Even the wicked bull, of whom stalwart boys were afraid, obeyed when Bára shook her fist at him.

When Jacob wished to take the herd out to wade or to drive them across the river he would place Bára on the back of one of the cows and say, "Hold on!" He himself would swim across after the herd. Once Bára was not holding tight and slipped off into the water. Lišaj pulled her out by the skirt and her father gave her a good scolding. She asked her father then what a person must do in order to swim. Her father showed her how to move arms and legs, and Bára remembered it and tried to hold herself above the water until she learned how to swim. She enjoyed swimming so much that in the summertime both morning and evening she would go in bathing and was able not only to keep her head above water, but to swim with her head under water. However, no one beside her father knew of her ability in this respect. From dawn until ten o'clock at night there was not a time when Bára had not gone in swimming, yet she had never seen the "water-man," and therefore she had no faith in his existence nor did she fear the water.

In broad midday and also at full midnight Bára had been out under the clear skies and had seen neither noon nor night specters. In the summer she liked to sleep in the stall beside the open dormer window, and yet nothing unusual had ever appeared before her to frighten her.

Once when she was out herding and was lying under

"BEWITCHED BÁRA" 159

a tree at the edge of the wood with Lišaj near her she recalled the tale of the traveler who, like her, lay under a tree in the forest and wished himself in a palace beside a beautiful princess, and to attain his desire wanted to sell himself to the devil. Barely did his thoughts turn to the devil when the devil stood before him

"What would I wish for if the devil appeared before me now?" Bára asked herself, patting Lišaj's head.

"Hm!" she smiled. "I'd ask him to give me such a headkerchief that when I'd wrap myself in it I'd be invisible and when I'd say, 'Take me to such and such a place,' I'd be there at once. I'd first of all want to be with Elška." And she thought hard a long, long time, but it was quiet everywhere, not even a tree rustling. Finally her curiosity gave her no peace and she called out softly, "Mr. Devil!"

Not a sound in response.

Then a little louder and more and more loudly until her voice re-echoed far and wide, "Devil, Mr. Devil!" Among the herd the black heifer raised its head, and when the voice sounded again it separated from the rest of the cattle and ran merrily to the forest. Then Lišaj leaped up, intending to return the heifer to the herd as was his duty. The black heifer stood still.

Bára burst into gay laughter. "Leave it alone, Lišaj. The heifer is obedient and thought I was calling it." She jumped up, patted the "devil" on the neck and from that time believed no more in tales of demons.

Near the wood, several hundred steps beyond the river, was a cemetery. After prayers the people did not like to go in that direction. There were many weird tales of dead men who roved about at midnight. But Bára passed that way many a time at night and never yet had she met with any fearful experience. She did not, therefore, believe that the dead arise and dance on their own graves or go about scaring people.

When the young people went out into the forest to gather strawberries or juniper berries and came upon a snake there was always a great scurrying. If the snake lifted its head and showed its fangs they all ran to the water, believing if they could reach it first the snake would be deprived of all power.

Bára never ran away. She was not afraid of a wicked bull, and therefore much less of a snake or a scorpion. If it lay in her path, she drove it away. If it refused to move and defended itself, she killed it. If it did not obstruct her path, she left it alone.

In short, Bára did not know fear or dread. Even when the thunder rolled and the storm poured forth its wrath over the valley Bára never trembled. On the contrary, when the villagers closed their windows and doors, lighted the consecrated Candlemas candles and prayed in fear and trembling lest the Lord be angry with them, Bára delighted in standing out on the boundary ridge the better to view the horizon spread out before her eyes.

Jacob often said to her, "I don't understand, girl, what joy you can have to look into the heavens when God is angry."

"Just the same sort of joy I have as when he smiles," she answered. "Just see, father, that fire—how beautiful it is amid the black clouds!"

"Don't point!" shrieked Jacob warningly. "God's messenger will break off your finger! He who does not fear the tempest has no fear of the Lord, don't you know that?"

"Elška of the parsonage once read me out of a book that we must not fear a storm as if it were the wrath of God, but that we should admire in it His divine power. The priest always preaches that God is only good and is love wholly. How could it be that He is so often angry at us? I love God and so I'm not afraid of His messenger."

Jacob disliked long speeches and so he left Bára to her own thinking. The neighbors, however, seeing the girl's fearlessness and that nothing evil occurred to her, were all the more convinced that she was a child protected by some supernatural power.

Besides her father, Elška and Josífek, who were of her own age, were the only ones who loved her. Josífek was the son of the sexton, Elška was the niece of the parish priest. Josífek was a lad of slender build, pale, golden-haired, good-hearted, but very timid.

Bára was a head taller than he, and when there was a fight, Josífek always hid behind her skirts, for Bára always courageously took his part against the boys for whom he alone was no match. For that Josífek loved her very dearly, brought her dried apples and every Saturday a white wafer-cake. One Sunday when Bára was still quite small he brought her home with him, intending to show her a little altar he had there and how well he could act the part of a priest. They went along hand in hand with Lišaj lagging on behind.

The doors of all the peasant homes closed with a latch and at night were bolted. At the parsonage the iron-cased oak doors were always locked and whoever wished to enter had to ring. At the sexton's there was also a bell, just as at the parsonage, and often the village youths, when passing, would open the door a little in order to hear the bell ring and the sexton's wife scold. When she had had her fill of railing at them they yelled, "Vixen, vixen!" at her.

When Bára with Josífek entered the door and the bell sounded, the sexton's wife ran out into the passageway. The end of her long nose was pinched up in a pair of spectacles and she cried out in a snuffling voice, "Who is this you're bringing with you?" Josífek stood as if scalded, dropped his eyes and was silent. Bára also looked down and said nothing. But behind the sexton's wife came running the tom-cat and, catching sight of Lišaj, began to bristle up its back, sputter and

"BEWITCHED BÁRA" 163

glare furiously. Lišaj began to growl, then barked and started after the cat. The cat leaped up on the cupboard and when Lišaj tried to follow it even there it jumped up on the shelves among the pans. That was as far as it could reach, but every hair stood on end with anger. Lišaj continued to leap up awkwardly on the shelving and barked deafeningly. The sexton ran out to learn the cause of the commotion, and beheld the foes in combat and his furious wife. He himself flew into a rage and, opening the door, shrieked at the children, "Get out of here right away with that beast and stay where you came from!"

Bára didn't let herself be ordered twice, and, calling Lišaj whom the sexton struck smartly with a cane, she ran as if from a fire. Josífek called her back, but she shook her head, saying, "Even if you'd give me a heifer, I'll never go back to your house." And she kept her word, even though Josífek persistently pleaded and promised that his mother would be glad to see her if she'd leave the dog at home. Never would she consent to step in the house again, and from that time, too, she lost all respect and love for everything smacking of the sexton—with the exception of Josífek. She had always thought the sexton on an equality with the priest and had the greatest esteem for him, for he dressed like the priest and in church had everything under his command. When he boxed the ears of some mischievous boy in church there dared not be even a murmur, and the neighbors, when they wanted something of the priest, always stopped first for advice at the sexton's.

"The sexton must indeed be a worthy person," the girl had always thought, but from the time that he so rudely showed her the door and struck Lišaj so smartly that, whimpering, he hopped on three legs all the way home, she always thought to herself, "You are not good at all," whenever she met him.

How different it all was when Elška took Bára home with her to the parsonage every Thursday and Sunday. The moment the doorbell rang the maid would open the door and admit the two girls and also Lišaj, for their own dog got along well with him. Softly the two girls would go to the servants' hall, climb up over the oven where Elška had her toys and dolls. The priest, who was an old man, used to sit on a bench at the table, and with his snuff-box and blue pocket handkerchief lying before him always dozed with his head leaning against the wall. Only once had he been awake; and when Bára ran to him to kiss his hand he patted her head, saying: "You're a good little girl. Run away and play together now, my little maids!"

Also Miss Pepinka, the priest's sister, was kind. She had no extensive conversation with Bára, although she liked to talk a good deal to the neighbor women, but she always gave her a big piece of bread with honey or a large muffin for lunch, larger than to Elška. Miss Pepinka was a short, little person who was taking on fat with the years. She was rosy, had a mole on her chin and rather weepy eyes, but in her youthful years, as she said herself, she used to be pretty, to which statement the sexton always nodded assent. She wore a long dress after the fashion of city women, with a short waist, an immense apron with large pockets, and at her side always dangled a bunch of keys. Her gray hair was always smooth, and on week days she wore a brown headkerchief with a yellow border, whereas on Sundays the headkerchief was yellow with a brown border. Miss Pepinka usually was busy with something around the house or in the field, spinning or, with her glasses on her nose, patching things. Sunday afternoons after dinner she, too, would doze a little, and after vespers she would play cards with her brother and the sexton. She rarely addressed him as "brother" but usually "Reverend Sir."

Miss Pepinka was the head of the house and what she wanted was carried out. What she said counted as unmistakable truth in the house, and when she favored anyone, all favored him.

Elška was the pet of both Miss Pepinka and the reverend father, and what Elška wished, that, too was desired by Miss Pepinka. Whom Elška loved was in Pepinka's good graces. Therefore Bára never received an unkind glance at the parsonage and Lišaj, too, was tolerated. The sexton, who could not endure dogs, often tried to pat Lišaj, in order to curry favor, but Lišaj, who could not bear the sexton, invariably snarled at him.

Bára was wholly happy when she could be at the parsonage. In the rooms everything fairly glistened. There were beds piled with fine bedding to the very ceiling, many beautiful pictures, and inlaid cabinets. In the garden were many flowers, vegetables and fine fruit. In the yard was poultry of all kinds; in the stable, cattle which it was a pleasure to look at. The herdsman Jacob had the greatest delight in the cattle belonging to the parish. And in the servants' hall, over the oven, what a quantity of toys! Elška never mixed up mud cakes nor played with brick dust and lime. She always had real cooking things and what was prepared was also eaten.

Why shouldn't Bára have been happy in such a home? But to her, Elška herself was far dearer than anything else. Oftentimes it seemed to her that she loved Elška more than she did her own father. If Elška had lived even in the flax-house, Bára would, nevertheless, have loved to be with her. Elška never once laughed at Bára and when she had anything she always shared it with her. Often she would throw her arms around Bára's neck and say, "Bára, I like you so very much."

"She likes me so much, and yet she is so beautiful and belongs at the parsonage. All the people address her as 'you' and not 'thou,' even the schoolmaster and sexton. All others mock at me," Bára repeated to

"BEWITCHED BÁRA" 167

herself, and in spirit she always embraced and kissed Elška for her friendship, though in reality she timidly refrained from expressing, as she longed to do, her fervent feeling.

When they were running about on the meadow and Elška's braid became loosened Bára pleaded: "Elška, let me braid it. You have hair as fine as flax. I love to braid it." At her willing consent, Bára delighted to play with the soft strands of hair and admire its beauty. After plaiting it, she pulled down her own braid and, placing it beside Elška's, said, "What a difference." True enough, Elška's hair beside Bára's resembled gold beside hardened steel. But yet Elška was not satisfied with it and wished she might have hair that was black like Bára's.

Sometimes when Elška came over to Bára's and they were certain that no one saw them they went in bathing. Elška, however, was timid, and no matter how much Bára assured her that nothing would happen and that she'd hold her and teach her to swim, still she would never go into water deeper than to her knees. After their bath Bára liked to wipe Elška's feet with her coarse apron and, clasping the tiny white feet in her strong palms, she kissed them and said with laughter: "Lord, but your feet are tender and small! What would happen if you had to walk barefoot. Look!" she added, comparing her own sun-browned, bruised feet full of callouses with Elška's dainty white ones.

"Doesn't it hurt you?" asked Elška, rubbing her

hand on the hard lower surface of Bára's feet with sympathetic touch.

"Until the skin became like sole-leather my feet used to hurt, but now I don't even feel fire beneath them," Bára answered with pride, and Elška wondered greatly. Thus the two girls enjoyed each other. Often Josífek joined them, and when they were preparing feasts he had to bring what was needed and did the slicing and the grating. When they played wolf, he had to be the lamb, and when the game was barter, he had to haul the pots and kettles. But he never objected, and liked best to play with the girls.

The twelfth year passed over the heads of the children and there was an end to their childish joys. The sexton put Josífek in a school in the city, as he wanted to make a priest of him. Miss Pepinka took Elška to Prague to a rich, childless aunt, in order that Elška should learn city manners and that the aunt should not forget her country relatives. Bára remained alone with her father and Lišaj.

II

Life in the rural districts flows along softly without noise or rustle, like a meadow brook. Three years had passed since Elška had gone away to Prague. At first neither Miss Pepinka nor the priest could become accustomed to her absence and were very lonely for her. When, however, the sexton reminded them why they had sent Elška from home, Miss Pepinka always said, very sententiously: "My dear Vlček, man must not live for today, we must think for the future. We—God granting—will get through life somehow, but Elška is young and that we must keep in mind. To save money—how in the name of the dear God can we do it—when we have none! Some feather-beds, her dowry—that is all she will have as an inheritance from us—and that is very little. The world takes note of these (and at this Pepinka opened her palm and with her other hand went through the pantomime of counting coins)—and her Prague aunt has countless numbers of them. Maybe Elška will win her favor. It is only for her own good that we are leaving her there."

The sexton acquiesced in every particular.

The Prague aunt had been ill for years. From the time of her husband's death she always wrote to her brother-in-law and sister-in-law that she had been kept alive only by medicines and if her physician did not thoroughly understand her constitution she would long ago be lying in the holy field. Suddenly, however, Elška wrote that her aunt had a new physician who had advised that she take a daily bath in cold water, walk a great deal, eat and drink heartily, and that she would soon be cured. Her aunt had obeyed and was now as healthy as a lynx.

"Hm, such new-fangled treatments. If that's the case, Elška can come home at once." All Miss Pepinka ordered was faithfully carried out. That very day the hostler had to pull out the carriage from the shed and take it to the wheelwright. Miss Pepinka, having decided to herself escort Elška, brought out her hat from the small chamber for inspection to see if it had suffered any damage. Yes, Miss Pepinka also had a hat which she had received ten years ago when she was in Prague, from that same aunt. In the village of Vestec no one had ever beheld her in it, but when she went on a pilgrimage with her brother to the deanery in a nearby town she put it on, and now when she was going to Prague she took it along in order, she said, not to disgrace the aunt by wearing a kerchief on her head.

The next day the carriage was repaired and the third day Pepinka ordered that it be well greased and the horses shod. On the fourth day she ceased household duties and sent for Bára to look after things during her absence. On the fifth day early in the morning they piled into the carriage fodder for the horses, food for the coachman and also for Miss Pepinka herself, a basket of eggs, a jar of butter and similar gifts for the aunt, the box with the hat, a bundle of clothes, and after holy mass Miss Pepinka herself, after long parting injunctions, stowed herself away inside. The coachman whipped up the horses and, putting themselves in God's hands, they started on their journey. Whoever saw the antiquated carriage which resembled a winged caldron hanging amid four wheels doffed his hat from afar, although Miss Pepinka herself, wrapped in numerous shawls, in the depths of the vehicle among all sorts of articles, including a pile of hay towering above her, was wholly invisible. But the peasants recognized the equipage, their fathers, too, had known it, and they used to say among themselves that that carriage remembered Žižka.

No one more ardently looked forward to Elška's arrival than Bára. No one thought so fervently of her, no one spoke of her oftener. When she had no one to talk with she conversed with Lišaj and promised him good times when Elška would return and asked him if he, too, did not yearn for her. Miss Pepinka and the good priest knew how much Bára loved Elška and they liked her the more for it. Once when Miss Pepinka had been slightly ill, and Bára with greatest willingness was waiting on her, she became so convinced of the girl's loyalty and good heart that she often called her in afterwards to help her. At last she reposed so much faith in her that she entrusted to her care the key to the larder, which in Miss Pepinka's own eyes was the highest evidence of favor. That is why she put the whole household into Bára's hands, on her departure, at which all the housekeepers in the village wondered greatly. Pepinka's mark of preference aroused greater antipathy than ever in the sexton's wife against Bára. The gossips said immediately: "See, such good-for-nothings have luck from hell—. She has nested herself securely at the parsonage." By which they meant Bára. Prejudice against the girl had not died out. She herself did not worry whether or not people liked her. She did not push herself forward among the young people either in playing or dancing, but attended to her own affairs and to her old father. The parsonage was her Prague.

There were some voices in the village which said: "One must give the girl all honor as having skill and strength which no girl and very few men can equal. What girl can carry two buckets full of water and yet walk as if she were toying with them? And who can look after a herd as she can? A horse or bull, a cow or sheep, all obey her, she controls all of them. Such a girl is a real blessing in a household." But if a youth here or there announced, "I'd like to make her my wife," the mothers at once shrieked, "No, no, my boy! Don't bring that girl into our family. No man can say how things will turn out with her. She is the wild sort—bewitched!"

And so none of the boys were permitted to court her seriously, and to attempt it in sport no one of them dared. Bára would not let herself be ruled nor would she be blinded by flattering words. The sexton's wife hated her most of all, although Bára never laid so much as a straw across her path. Indeed, on the contrary, she did good by protecting Josífek from the revenge of the boys. Whenever any boy got a box on the ear in church from the sexton he always tried to return it to Josífek. But the sexton's wife was angry at Josífek for being a dunce and permitting a girl to defend him and for liking that girl. She was angry

"BEWITCHED BÁRA" 173

because Bára went often to the parsonage and because they liked her there. She would have forced her out of the parsonage if Miss Pepinka had been anyone but Miss Pepinka, but the latter did not permit others to blow on her mush and least of all the sexton's wife. Once on a time this worthy, together with the wife of the schoolmaster, had made up some gossip about Miss Pepinka and from that time their friendship ceased, although formerly they had been together constantly. Miss Pepinka often taunted Mr. Vlček with it, saying, "A sharp nose likes to pry," which referred to the sexton's wife. Vlček was a lamb at the parsonage and only at home was he a real wolf.

Two, three, four days passed since Pepinka had left and Bára could hardly wait.

"Good sir, how far is it to Prague?" she said to the priest when he had had his afternoon nap and was in his best humor.

"Be patient, girl. They can't be back yet. A hundred miles—that's some distance. Three days to get there, two days Pepinka will stop in Prague, and three days for the return trip—figure it up yourself!"

Bára counted the days, and when the fourth day after the conversation arrived there were great preparations at the parish house, and then Bára counted only the hours. For the tenth time she rushed out to look down the road. The sun was already sinking and her father was driving home the herd when the carriage appeared on the highway.

"They are coming," shouted Bára, so that it could be heard over the whole place. The priest went out in front of the gate and the sexton after him. Bára would like to have flown directly to them, but she became shy suddenly and only ran about from place to place. When the carriage neared the parsonage a sort of fear filled her, her heart pounded, her throat contracted and heat and cold surged over her.

The carriage stopped at the gate. First, Miss Pepinka rolled out of it and behind her leaped forth the slender figure of a rosy-cheeked girl upon whom the priest, the sexton and the assembled crowd stood gazing. If she had not thrown her arms around the priest's neck and called him "Uncle" they would not have believed it was Elška.

Bára never took her eyes from her. When Elška emerged from her uncle's embrace she stepped at once to Bára, took her two hands in her own and, looking up into her eyes, said in her sweet voice, "Bára, Bára—I've been so lonely for you! How have you been? Is Lišaj still alive?" Then Bára burst into tears and cried as if her heart would break, unable to answer a word. After a while she sighed gratefully, "Well, it's good that you are here at last, dear Elška!"

The priest repeated after Bára: "Well, it's good that you are here. We've been so lonely."

"They wanted to detain me there a day longer," said Miss Pepinka, piling all sorts of things out of the carriage into the arms of the sexton, Bára and the

"BEWITCHED BÁRA"

maid. "But I was worried, dear brother, about you. I didn't want you to be alone, and besides we wouldn't have had enough feed for the horses," she added.

They put the old equipage back for a rest into the carriage-house, Miss Pepinka laid away her hat in the little room as spotless as when she took it out, disposed of what she had brought with her and distributed the gifts. Bára received a lovely ribbon for her skirt and one for her hair, and from Elška a string of corals for her neck. Elška brought with her some beautiful dresses, but these would not have made her pleasing if she had not brought back with her from Prague her unspoiled good heart. She had not changed.

"Oh, Bára, you've grown up so!" was the first thing that Elška wondered at when she had time to talk to Bára and inspect her properly.

Bára had grown a head taller than Elška.

"Oh, Elška, you are just as good as you always were, only so much prettier. If it wouldn't be a sin, I'd say that you look like the Virgin Mary on our altar."

"Oh, there—there! What are you talking about," Elška rebuked her—but not at all severely. "You are flattering me."

"God forbid! I am telling you what my heart says. I can't get my fill of looking at you," Bára earnestly insisted.

"Dear Bára, if you'd only go to Prague! There you'd see the lovely girls!"

"More beautiful than you?" marvelled Bára.

"Yes, indeed. Far more beautiful," sighed Elška.

"Are there good people in Prague? Is it a beautiful place? Did you like it there?" questioned Bára a little later.

"They were all good to me, auntie, the governess,—all of them liked me. I liked to be among them all, but I longed so for you and kept wishing that you were there with me. Oh, Bára, dear, it is so beautiful there that you cannot even picture it in imagination. When I saw the Vltava, the beautiful churches, the huge buildings, the parks—I was as if struck dumb. And there were so many people on the streets as if there were a procession, some of them dressed in holiday costume even on the week days, carriages driving by constantly, turmoil and noise so that a person doesn't know who is with them. Just wait. Next year you and I will go there together to a church pilgrimage," added Elška.

"What would I do there? People would laugh at me!" said Bára.

"Don't believe it, dear. There, on the streets one person doesn't notice another, one doesn't even greet another in passing."

"I wouldn't like that. That must be a strange world," Bára wondered.

The next day—Sunday—Elška arrayed herself in her holiday clothes, placed on her head a very becoming red velvet cap such as was just in fashion, and went to early mass. All eyes in church were turned towards

"BEWITCHED BÁRA" 177

her and many a young man thought, "For you I'd serve even twice seven years if I knew I'd surely get you."

Whenever Elška was in church she was always devout and never looked about her and this time she was the same. But when she went from the church through the village she turned in all directions, greeting the villagers who crowded to her to welcome her home from Prague, inquired how each had been during her absence and answering their many questions. Many things had changed in those three years, although it hardly seemed so to the villagers. Here and there some aged man or old grandmother whom Elška had been accustomed to seeing on Sundays sitting on the high walk around their houses or in the orchard, warming themselves in the sun, was no more. In the circle of young people many a pair was missing, looking after their own newly established housekeeping. Children rolled in the grass whom Elška did not know. Many a head which had been gray was now white and the girls of Elška's own age were now being escorted by youths and were no longer regarded as children. And, too, no one addressed her now as "Elška," but all added to her name, "Maiden."

When Elška heard herself so addressed her cheeks flushed red. By this prefix the simple villagers expressed what she herself was scarcely conscious of— that she was no more a child. In Prague they had called her "the little miss" and later "miss." At first she had thought it was some sort of mockery, but hearing that it was the general title for girls, she accepted the custom. The title "Panna" or "Maiden" honored her more highly, expressing, as it did, virginity, and it was because she appreciated this that the blush of virgin shyness overspread her sweet face.

The sexton's wife also emerged to her threshold, and when Elška passed, invited her in. She liked Elška, though she thoroughly disliked Miss Pepinka. She asked Elška how she had liked it in Prague and how the altar of St. John looked at the castle and if it is true that the bridge is paved with gold. When Elška answered all these questions she examined her from head to foot, not even a thread escaping those venomous eyes. Elška asked about Josífek.

"Oh, he is getting along well in his studies. He is the best student in school and is growing like a reed out of the water. Many—ah—many times he asked about you, Maid Elška, when he was here for the holidays. He pined for you and had no one at all with whom to enjoy himself. With the local youth—it is not fitting for him to associate now that he is a student," said the sexton's wife.

Elška was of a different mind, but she said nothing.

In the afternoon Elška went to visit Bára. The shepherd's home was a little cottage, the smallest in the entire village, but, excepting the parsonage alone, there was nowhere greater cleanliness and neatness. A table, bench, two chairs, the beds, chest and loom formed its entire furniture, but all were as shining as glass. The walls were as white as chalk, the ceiling was scrubbed till it glistened as if made of polished walnut. On the walls were several pictures and over them green sprigs. On the shelves shone several pitchers and plates, all keepsakes left of her mother's dowry. The little windows were wide open all summer and on the sills stood pots of basil, sweet violets and rosemary. The floor was not boarded, consisting only of hardened thrashings, but Bára covered it with a rush-mat which she herself had woven.

Near the cottage there was a strip of orchard and a little flower-garden which Bára cultivated. Everywhere it was evident that the occupants of the cottage had few wants, but that the being who ruled it was not at all lacking in a sense of beauty.

Not a single girl in the village, not even excepting the maidservants, dressed as simply as did Bára, but not one of them looked as clean at her work, day in and day out, as Bára did. Her blouse, gathered at the neck and at the wrists, was of coarse cloth, but it was always as white as the fallen snow. This and her dark woolen skirt, her apron, also of coarse linen, formed her entire costume. On Sundays she put on shoes and wore a close-fitting bodice and in the winter she added a wool jacket. For ornamentation she wore a border on her skirt, red strings on her apron and red ribbons on her black braids which hung down on her back to her knees. The girls sometimes chided her for not wearing a tight girdle during the week, but she answered that she felt freer without and Elška always told her she looked better without a corset. There is no person free of some form of vanity and even Bára was not exempt.

Great was Bára's delight that Elška had come for a visit. She led her everywhere over the place, showing off her garden, the orchard, the field, and taking her out to the meadow to her father, who could not admire Elška enough, and wonder at how she had grown. In short they visited every spot where three years ago they had romped together. Then they sat down in the orchard. Bára brought a dish of cream in which black bread was crumbled, set it on the grass and with Elška ate it just as in former days. While they ate, Bára related things about her black cow, about Lišaj, and finally the conversation drifted to Josífek.

"Does Mrs. Vlček still dislike you?" asked Elška.

"Yes, indeed! When I'm around it is like salt in her eyes. When she knows nothing more slanderous to say of me she criticizes my eyes, saying that I look like a tadpole."

"How wicked of her!" Elška exclaimed angrily.

"Yes, truly, for I have never injured her in any way. The other day, though, I got angry about it. I sent her a mirror so that she might first look at her own beauty before she found fault with others' looks."

"You did just the right thing," laughed Elška. "But why does she hate you so?"

"BEWITCHED BÁRA" 181

"Oh, she's a hard one. She stings everyone with her basilisk eye, not only me. Perhaps she dislikes me because I am in better standing with your people than is Josífek and because Josífek likes me. The poor fellow gets a beating every time his mother learns that he has been to see me. I always tell him not to come here, but he comes anyway, and I am not to blame."

Elška was silent, but after a pause asked, "And do you like Josífek?"

"Why shouldn't I like him? Everybody picks on him just as they do on me. Poor little fellow! He can't defend himself and I feel sorry for him."

"Why, is he still the same as he used to be? Mrs. Vlček told me he had grown remarkably."

"Yes, as high as Lišaj's garters," smiled Bára. But at once she added compassionately, "How can he grow when his mother gives him more thumps on the back than she puts biscuits in his stomach?"

"And what does Vlček say to all that? It's his son, too!"

"Vlček and Mrs. Vlček are of one stripe. They are angry because Josífek does not want to become a priest. In the name of the Lord, how can he help it that he doesn't like it any more? Unwilling service surely could not be pleasing to God."

"Truly, it could not be," Elška confirmed.

A little while longer the girls talked, and then Bára accompanied Elška home. From that time they visited each other regularly as before, although they no longer played with dolls in the space over the oven.

But the friendship of the two girls did not suit the neighbor women. They began to gossip that it was odd that Elška should associate with the shepherd's daughter, that it was not fitting for her, that she should rather seek the society of the daughters of the mayor, the justice and others. Purposely, they said these things openly so that they would be carried to Miss Pepinka's ears. The talk vexed Miss Pepinka. It was not wise to irritate the neighbor women, yet Miss Pepinka did not like to send Elška among the local young people. Somehow it did not seem proper to invite the village girls to the parsonage when Elška did not herself seek them. She talked to Elška about it, and the latter briefly decided that she would sometimes go to visit the village girls, but that Bára would remain the dearest friend of her choice.

Miss Pepinka did not oppose this plan, for she liked Bára herself for many reasons. She thought that Bára would hardly be likely to marry and that later on she would become her right hand, after Elška married. Miss Pepinka had a suitor for Elška up her sleeve, so to speak, but no one knew of it, not even the priest. This suitor was the manager or steward on a nearby noble estate, who was pleasing to Miss Pepinka, and it seemed to her that it would be a very convenient arrangement for Elška's future. The manorial fields bordered on the parish lands and the steward,

"BEWITCHED BÁRA" 183

whenever he visited that section of the estate, always stopped at the parish house.

Elška had not an inkling of the happiness her aunt was in spirit preparing for her, and through her head flitted altogether different plans than any idea of becoming the wife of the steward. She had not yet told these plans even to Bára. But Bára often beheld Elška lost in thought and downcast, and from this she judged that something was weighing on her heart. Still she said nothing, thinking to herself, "When the right time comes, she will tell me."

Bára was not mistaken. Despite the fact that the neighbors tried to present Bára in an evil light to Elška and accused her of being unrestrained, still Elška believed in her more than in them all and cared for her in the same way as before. On the eve before St. John the Baptist's day the girls met and Elška asked Bára, "Are you going to toss a wreath tomorrow?"

"Alone, I wouldn't care to toss one, but if you wish to, come over before sunrise and we'll go together."

"I'll come!"

In the morning before the sun came up Elška already stood in the herdsman's orchard with Bára beside her. They were weaving white, blue and red blossoms on hoops made of willow twigs.

"Whom are you going to think of when you throw the wreath?" Elška asked of Bára.

"Dear Lord, I haven't any one to think of!" sighed

the girl. "I'll cast the wreath at random to see if it floats after yours. I only wish that when you marry, Elška, I could go with you."

Elška became silent as a blush overspread her cheeks. After a pause she said, extending her hand to Bára: "Here is my hand on it that we shall stay together; if you do not marry, I shall never marry," she added with a deep sigh.

"What are you saying, Elška? Very few people love me, but everyone cares for you. You will be rich; I am poor. You are beautiful and I am homely. You are well educated and I am a simple, stupid girl— and I am to think of a husband, and you not?"

"Auntie has always told me that it all depends on taste. To one a carnation is most becoming, to another a rose, to a third a violet. Every flower finds its own admirer, each has its own kind of beauty. Do not underrate yourself nor overvalue me; we are equals. Aren't you truly going to think of any of the boys, or haven't you thought of any as yet?"

"No, no," Bára shook her head, smilingly. "I don't think of any of them, and when they come a-courting I make short work of them. Why should I spoil my thoughts, or bind up my golden freedom?"

"But if one of them loved you very much and you him, then you'd let yourself be bound, wouldn't you?" asked Elška.

"Why, Elška, don't you know how it goes? First, his parents would bargain with my father and haggle

"BEWITCHED BÁRA"

about how much he would give me before their son would dare to marry me. My dowry isn't big enough to satisfy any parents I know, and I have no desire to be permitted to enter a household as a gracious act of favor. I would rather tie a millstone around my neck and jump into the river. If I'd voluntarily put a load on myself, I'd have to call myself a fool. If they abuse me now, they'd revile me doubly afterwards.

> 'And no matter what I am,
> I have a bouquet at my belt,'"

she finished, quoting the popular song as she placed at her waist a nosegay made of the surplus flowers from the wreath. Then pointing to the beams of the rising sun she cried, "We have no time to spare!"

Elška quickly finished weaving her wreath and both girls hastened to the nearby bridge which led over the river to the meadow. In the center of the bridge, they paused.

"Let's throw them together!" said Elška, lifting the wreath high above her head.

"All right! Ready!" cried Bára, tossing the wreath out over the water. But her wreath, cast by a strong arm, did not reach the water, but remained hanging on a willow. For an instant Bára stood in startled silence, then she wept. Finally she tossed her head resolutely, saying: "Well, let it hang there. The flowers look pretty up on that willow."

Elška, however, never removed her eyes from her

wreath, which, dropped by her trembling fingers, whirled a moment in one place in the river, then a wave seized it, pushed it on to a second, and that one to a third, and then carried it further and further down stream till it had vanished from the sight of the two girls.

Elška, with clasped hands on the railing of the bridge, gazed with flaming eye and cheek after the wreath now carried by a strong current. Bára, leaning against the rail, also looked silently after it.

"And your wreath was caught here. See, you will marry someone right here!" exclaimed Elška turning to Bára.

"According to that, it looks as if we weren't to be together, after all. I am to stay here and you are to go far away from us. But I don't believe in it. Man plans but God decrees."

"Of course," Elška said in a voice half sad, and dropped her eyes with a sigh to the stream below.

"So, then, Elška, you'd like to go far away from us? Don't you like it here?" asked Bára, and her dark-blue eyes gazed into Elška's face searchingly.

"Why, what are you thinking of?" whispered Elška, not raising her eyes. "I like it here, but . . ."

"But out there far away is someone for whom you are yearning, whom you'd like to go to—isn't that so, Elška?" concluded Bára, and laying her brown hand on the girl's white shoulder she looked with a smile into her face.

"BEWITCHED BÁRA" 187

Elška lifted her eyes to Bára's, tried to smile, but at the same time burst into tears.

"If something weighs on you, confide in me. With me it will be as if buried in a grave," said Bára.

Elška without a word laid her head on Bára's shoulder, embraced her and then fell to weeping. Bára held her gently as a mother holds her babe, kissing her golden hair.

High above the heads of the girls the lark soared, singing, and above the summit of the green forests the sun was rising, pouring its golden glow over the emerald valley. Jacob came out in front of the cottage and the sound of the shepherd's horn reminded the girls it was time to go home.

"Along the way we can tell each other," said Bára, leading Elška by the hand from the bridge to the meadow path.

"But how did you guess it about me?" questioned Elška.

"Dear Lord, that's easy to know. You are often absorbed in thought, sometimes you're sad and then again your face fairly glows. As I watched you I knew at once that there was something ailing you. I guessed right."

"Only, I hope Auntie hasn't noticed anything and that she won't question me," said Elška anxiously. "She would be angry. He would not please her," she finished.

"Does she know him?"

"She saw him in Prague. He is the one who cured Auntie."

"That doctor? I see. You mentioned several times to me what a good man he was. But why doesn't Miss Pepinka like him?"

"I don't know. She just scolds about him and says he's distasteful to her," Elška related almost tearfully.

"Why, is he displeasing?"

"Oh, Bára!" sighed the girl. "A man as handsome as he is cannot be found in the whole countryside!"

"Perhaps he isn't rich?"

"Rich? That I don't know. But what of it? What do riches amount to?"

"That's true, but your auntie will want you to marry a wealthy man who will provide well for you."

"No, no, Bára. I won't marry anyone else. I'd rather die!"

"Well, it won't be as bad as that. And even if he isn't rich, Miss Pepinka and your uncle will listen to reason when you tell them—that you love him."

"I don't dare tell them. My Prague aunt forbade me to tell them, but she promised us that she'd take care for our happiness even if Auntie Pepinka should oppose it. A week ago he wrote me that next month we'd meet again."

"You write to each other?"

"It's this way—my Prague auntie can't write and is near-sighted. Hynek—that's his name—it's a pretty name, isn't it?"

"BEWITCHED BÁRA" 189

"Strange, I've never before heard such a name," said Bára; and Elška continued:

"Hynek offered to write letters for her to me. She wouldn't write oftener than once a year, but he urges her to always send some message. Uncle has been much surprised that Auntie writes so often."

"And how about it, when your uncle reads the letters?"

"Oh, my dear, we have that part all planned out. We write in such a way that no one can understand excepting we alone."

"After all, it's a fine thing when a person is accomplished. I'd never be able to do it."

"Oh, you'd learn that easily enough," said Elška. They had just reached the cottage, and she took both of Bára's hands and, looking with clear eyes into Bára's face, she said: "You can't even believe how much better and freer I feel now, as if a stone had fallen from my heart. Now I can talk to you about him. But," she added with a confidential tone in her voice, "you, Bára, have you nothing to tell me?"

"I?" stammered Bára, and her large eyes dropped. "I—nothing!"

"Just a little word?"

"Nothing, Elška, nothing. Mere dreams!"

"Tell them to me, then!"

"Some other time!' Bára shook her head, slipped her hands out of Elška's grasp and, pointing to the stable and the doghouse, concluded, "Look, Lišaj is chafing to be out and Blackie will hang herself. It's time to let them out. And your cows are already in the herd; I hear their bells. In a minute father will drive them past. Go past the garden, Elška, so that the peasant women wouldn't see you and gossip about you!"

"Oh, let them talk. I'm doing nothing wrong. But I'll mind you. I'm going, but just as soon as possible we must tell each other more," said Elška as she disappeared between the hedges.

III

Two rumors were being carried about the village. On every estate, in every cottage nothing else was talked of than the ghost in the parish forest and the approaching marriage of Maid Elška and the steward.

"So she forgot her first love thus early?" the reader will think. Do not wrong Elška. She had not proved disloyal in even a thought and had determined to undergo anything before she would become the steward's wife. Even if she were not already betrothed, the steward was by no means the sort of man with whom she could have fallen in love.

He was of a short figure, as if he had been baked and set up on two short legs. His cheeks were as red as peonies, as was his nose also. On his head was a round bald spot which, however, he sought to cover with the red hair which still remained around his ears and neck. His eyes were surrounded by flabby fat and had the peculiar quality, especially for a steward, that at one and the same time they looked in two different directions. In the summer he wore a straw hat with a green ribbon, a cane with a tassel, nankeens, a winter double-breasted vest so that he wouldn't take cold or get his shirt soiled, a cotton kerchief around his neck, and a clove-colored frock-coat with pointed tail and yellow buttons. From his pocket usually hung the corner of a blue handkerchief, for the steward used snuff.

It was said among the peasants of Vestec that the subjects of the neighboring manor had many a time dusted that clove-colored frock-coat with their sticks, but that somehow the matter never got to the courts. The steward was very timorous, but nevertheless the peasants were afraid of him, for he made up for his cowardliness by craft and revengefulness—with which he paid them back. To the people from whom he could expect any sort of benefit he was very fawning and polite, otherwise he was a very harsh man. He was also very stingy. The only good quality which no one could deny him was his wealth. Yes, indeed, the manager, Kilián Sláma, was a rich man, and that was the quality in him which appealed to Miss Pepinka. For that matter, she did not mean that his figure was unhandsome—for she never did like tall, spare people. Besides, she was flattered because the steward always kissed her hand. She thought that in time he would find favor in Elška's eyes also, that she would get accustomed to him. She told her brother, who didn't want to hear of the plan, that such a man would value his wife more than could some young fop, and that he would carry out every wish of Elška's who would be a lady, well provided for and, should he die, there would be no worries about the future.

"And if my brother should die," she reasoned in her mind further, "I'll have a place to go."

In short, Miss Pepinka knew how to manage cleverly so that the steward visited the parish often, and finally even the priest made no further objection. The good pastor got accustomed to him and missed the steward when he did not come for supper and he had only Miss Pepinka and the sexton or the schoolmaster to play cards with. Elška at first had no idea of Pepinka's plan, and listened to praises of his goodness and wealth with about as much concern as she paid to his awkward enough courting. But the steward became more insistent, and her aunt more open in her designs until Elška comprehended fully. It amused her, but when her aunt made it clear that the matter was serious, reprimanding her severely, and when the priest counselled her to accept the steward, she began to be gloomy, to avoid the steward and to hasten with her burdens to Bára.

Bára learned Miss Pepinka's plan from the lady herself, for Pepinka wished her to aid in persuading Elška. But she struck the wrong note there, for even if Bára had not known of Elška's love she would not have tried to influence her. She herself esteemed the steward no more than the dust in her eyes and would not have accepted him even if he had offered her the entire noble estate. She said neither yes nor no to Miss Pepinka, but conspired secretly with Elška. She herself carried to the town post-office Elška's letter detailing everything fully to her Prague aunt.

From the time that Elška learned of the steward's intent he did not have a pleasant word or glance from her. No one would have said that the kind-hearted and always amiable Elška could speak sharply or frown. Whenever he approached the parish he heard in the village square or from some hedge abusive songs, as if composed and sung for him especially. He tolerated it all, however, except once when he met Bára and she began suddenly to sing—

> "Any sort of manikin,
> On spindly legs so thin
> Would like to choose our prettiest girl,
> It surely is a sin.—"

He nearly burst with bristling anger, and his nose crimsoned like a turkey gobbler's when it sees red. But what was the use? The steward had already swallowed all sorts of shaming and mockery—so he gulped down the teasing of the girls, thinking to himself, "Just wait, my girl, until I have you and your money—then I'll show them all what's what!" But the steward forgot that even in Stupidville they don't hang a thief until they catch him.

One morning it was told around through the village that a ghost had been seen. A woman in white had gone from the parish forest to the village, through the square, over the meadows and somewhere near the graveyard had mysteriously disappeared. The sexton's wife fell sick of fright, for, she said, the ghost had rapped on her window, and when the sexton stepped to the window, not knowing who it was, he beheld a white specter surmounted by a skull and it made a wry face at him, while the figure shook its finger threateningly. It was a wonder Vlček himself did not become ill as a result, but the sexton's wife would have it that death had given her warning that in a year and a day she must die.

The night watchman also took his oath that it was a ghost and that it came out of the parish wood. People began to dig up past history, if perhaps someone had not hanged himself there, but when they could not think up any such incident they said that once upon a time someone buried a treasure somewhere and that his spirit had no peace and was seeking someone to free it. All sorts of conjectures were made and the talk was only of the specter.

"I don't believe it," said Bára to Elška when she came to her that same evening to the meadow near the wood where Jacob was pasturing the herd.

"Whether it's true or not, I'm grateful to the ghost, for it has rid me for several days of a much-disliked guest. To be sure, he wrote to uncle that they are having harvest and a great deal of work and that he cannot come for several days, but I'd wager my head that he heard about the specter and is afraid. He's a terrible coward and he has to come by way of the parish forest."

"I wish it had blown him away so that he'd come no more to Vestec. I'd rather see you in your coffin than with that bald-pate at the altar," Bára scolded. "I don't see where Miss Pepinka puts her reason that she forces you to accept such a creature. And yet she is a good woman."

"She thinks she is making provision for a comfortable future for me. That is the only reason I am not utterly angry at her, but I cannot marry him, no matter what happens."

"And you must not. God would punish you since you gave your promise to Mr. Hynek, if you did not keep it. You know the saying, 'He who breaks the vow of love, alas, alas, for his soul!'"

"I shall never, never break it even if it would take years," asserted Elška. "But he—he—if only he will not forget! In Prague there are beautiful girls who are his equals. But, Bára, if he would forget me I would grieve myself to death!" And Elška began sobbing.

"You are a foolish child to worry yourself so. Yesterday you told me what a fine man Mr. Hynek was and how much he loves you, and today you have doubts of him?"

Elška wiped her eyes, smiled and, throwing herself

down beside Bára on the grass, said: "It was only a passing thought. I believe in him as I do in God! Oh, if I were only that little bird and could fly to him and tell him all that grieves me!"

To Bára at once occurred the song, "If I were a nightingale!" and she began to sing, but it did not go merrily, for in the middle of the song she paused suddenly, as if terror-stricken. Her cheeks, too, became red.

"What frightened you? Why did you stop singing?" Elška asked, but Bára did not answer, only gazed off into the forest.

"Bára, Bára!" Elška shook her finger reproachfully. "You are hiding something from me and I haven't a secret thought before you. That isn't nice of you."

"I don't know myself what I'd say," replied Bára.

"Why did you start just now? You are never afraid of anything? Who was that in the forest?"

"A huntsman, perhaps," Bára said evasively.

"You know very well who it was. Your fright wasn't over nothing. Maybe it was the ghost you saw?"

"No, no! I wouldn't be afraid of that," laughed Bára heartily, and wished to change the subject, but Elška persisted in unreeling the same thread until finally she asked directly if Bára would marry Josífek in case he did not become a priest. Bára burst into even louder laughter than before.

'God save me!" she cried. "The sexton's wife

would cook up a snake for me the first day. Josífek is a good boy, but he doesn't fit among us. He is neither for the herd nor the plow, and it wouldn't be proper to put him at the spinning-wheel. Still I might keep him behind a frame and under glass for exhibition."

Elška, too, had to laugh at her notion, but after a while she asked Bára very earnestly, "Then there is truly no one whom you are fond of?"

"Listen, Elška!" Bára said, after short deliberation. "Last fall it happened often that alone with Lišaj I took the herd out. Father had a sore foot and could not stand up. One afternoon the mayor's cow, Plavka, and Milost's cow, Březina, got into a fight and began to gore each other with their horns. One must never let them get into a rage or they'd dig out each other's horns. So I seized a pail and ran to the river for some water to throw on their heads. Before I returned to the herd some huntsman approached from the wood and, seeing the cows with their locked horns, tried to drive them apart.

"Away— Go away!" I shrieked at him. "I'll separate them myself. Don't let the bull see you, he's wicked!" The huntsman turned around, but in that instant the bull, also, had caught sight of him. Luckily, the cows ran off in different directions when I splashed the water over them or it would have been hard for the huntsman to escape. It was all I could do to seize the bull, restrain and calm him, for even father can't hold him, though he usually obeys me when I threaten him. The huntsman hid himself in the wood behind a tree and watched. When the herd was again peacefully at pasture he appeared at the edge of the forest and asked me whose daughter I was. I told him. He looked at me strangely, doffed his cap, thanked me for my protection and went away into the forest. After that I saw him many times, but I never spoke with him again except to greet him when he passed near by. He used to stand on the edge of the wood or walk along the river's bank, even coming into the village, all that winter and spring. On St. John's day early in the morning after you left I was helping father drive out the cows when I saw him coming over the meadow to the bridge. He paused where you had stood, looked around, then stepped down from the bridge into the bushes near the bank. There I distinctly saw him take down my wreath which had remained hanging on the willow and hide it under his coat. Just a few moments ago I saw him down there near the wood. Why I always have a sudden fright whenever I see him, I don't know."

"And you truly have never talked with him?"

"Not a word more than at that first meeting," Bára declared.

"But you like him, don't you?" Elška questioned further.

"Yes, as I do every good man who has wronged no one."

"But you don't know whether he is good when you haven't talked with him."

"He certainly is not bad. It doesn't show in his eyes!"

"So you truly do like him?" Elška insisted searchingly.

"There are handsome boys in the village, but if you want the truth, I must say that no one of them pleases me as does he. I often dream of him!"

"What a person thinks of, that he dreams of."

"Oh, not always. Dreams also come from God."

"But tell me honestly—if that huntsman should say, 'Bára, I mean to marry you,' would you consent?"

"Elška, how you talk! He will never think of me, let alone wishing to marry me. Those are all vain dreams and speeches. Forget it all! Ho! Ho! Plavka, where are you going? Lišaj, where are you? Don't you see Plavka getting after Březina?" Bára interjected, leaping up from the soft green turf to turn aside the cow, meanwhile.

Whenever later Elška wanted to turn the conversation to the subject of the huntsman Bára always evaded her by beginning about Hynek. By that magic word she knew she could turn Elška from any subject.

A few days later the steward was again at the parish. Nothing had frightened him off. But—he came in the daytime. Even at the parsonage there was discussion of the ghost. While the priest had no faith in similar superstititions, still it was thought there was something to the tales, for every third night precisely from eleven to twelve it "haunted," according to the testimony of reputable people. It shook its fist at many a person and a death's head looked into numerous windows. The people were so terrified that only the boldest men ventured outside their own thresholds at night. They began repenting their sins and gave generously for prayers for souls in purgatory. In fact fear of death drove them all to do penance. To be sure, the priest preached against superstition and false beliefs, but it was all useless.

The steward, though he would not own to it, was so frightened that he visibly paled, and if it had not been for his great greed to possess a beautiful bride and her rich dowry, the parsonage would not have seen him again. He wanted, therefore, to have certainty assured as soon as possible. For that reason he had come to a definite understanding with Miss Pepinka and the priest and decided to consult even Elška so that the wedding could be celebrated immediately after harvesttime.

Miss Pepinka announced to Elška the steward's impending visit the next day and urged her to be sensible and listen to reason. Elška wept and begged her aunt not to force her to marry such a scarecrow, but Pepinka became very angry with her. Even her uncle, although he did not rebuke her as did his sister, nevertheless reproved her for ingratitude and unreasonableness. No letter came from Prague—and not a

"BEWITCHED BÁRA" 201

word of any news. Elška knew not what to do. She consulted Bára, who encouraged her to be brave and further incensed her against the steward, but all this was no real help to her.

The next day came—the day when the ghost did not haunt—and the steward arrived all dressed up in finery to do his courting. Miss Pepinka cooked and baked from earliest dawning in order the better to honor the guest. Even wine came to the table to celebrate the glorious day. Bára was also at the parish and only on her persuasion was Elška able to stand on her feet at all, for the whole affair made her terribly ill.

When he actually pressed his demands, Elška told him to come back a week later for her final word. She hoped against hope that in the meantime some word would come from Prague. The steward was not pleased with her evasive answer nor the cold demeanor of his bride-to-be, for he saw something was not right. But there was nothing to do but keep still and trust in his protectress, Miss Pepinka. Despite his chagrin, the food and drinks tasted excellently and his cheeks fairly burned. That day he wore a blue frock-coat so the contrast was all the more marked.

When evening approached, the steward wished to go home, but the priest did not wish to let him go yet. An hour later when he again spoke of going the priest said: "Just stay a little longer. Vlček will accompany you, and also the hostler. It's possible that some sort of rabble does infest our forest."

The steward acted as if some one had dashed ice-water over him. He no longer had any appetite and would have preferred to see himself at home in bed. The only thing that held him was the promise of having an escort. Vlček had a bit too much in his head and the stableman, too, had tippled, thinking to himself, "It doesn't happen every day," and neither cared to go until it was after ten. Then, at last, they set out on the journey. The steward, sobered by fear, observed that both his escorts were intoxicated. They reeled along the road, one zigzagging here and the other there. There was no speech to be had with them and the steward was in mortal anxiety, although he buoyed himself up with the hope that this was not the regular night for the specter to appear.

Alas! how he had looked forward to that day—for which he had had everything well figured out and now everything was botched.

The night was clear enough; one could see from the village to the forest. The travellers were quite near it when suddenly there issued forth a white figure, appearing to them immensely tall and came directly towards them. The steward shrieked and rolled to the ground like a log. The sexton, sobered in a twinkling, started on a run. Only the hostler remained standing like a pillar, but when the figure with skeleton white hand unveiled its head, showing a grinning skull, his hair stood on end and he fell to his knees down beside the steward. The figure, however, took no notice of him, but with a powerful grip lifted up the kneeling steward to his feet and shrieked in a hollow voice into his ear, "If you ever dare go a-courting again to the parsonage you sign your own death-warrant!" Without another word the weird apparition stalked with long, slow strides towards the village.

Meanwhile Vlček rushing, breathless, to the village square overtook the night watchman. Together they called out half the village. The more courageous ventured out, taking clubs and flails, while the sexton ran to the church to get some consecrated object.

They took him in their midst and started towards the parish wood. At the edge of the village they caught sight of the tall white specter striding along slowly, not to the town, but obliquely over the meadows towards the graveyard. For an instant they paused, but then with shouts encouraging each other to boldness they advanced in one body after the white figure which, observing them, speeded up its steps.

Suddenly, however, the specter began to run and on the bridge vanished completely from their eyes. They started after it now with more fearlessness. At the bridge they stopped.

"Something white is lying here!" they shouted.

The sexton made the sign of the cross above the bridge and when after pronouncing the words, "Praise ye all the good spirit of the Lord," no response was made, one of the peasants stepped closer and saw that it was only a dress lying there. With his club he raised the bundle gingerly, and carried it thus to the village. On their return they picked up the half-dead steward whom the hostler had to almost carry all the way back. They went directly to the parsonage.

The priest was not yet asleep and cheerfully opened the door. They there examined what they had found. All of them stood transfixed as if they had been dropped from the clouds. Two white sheets and a brown woollen skirt with a red border. They recognized the skirt.

"That belongs to bewitched Bára!" they all cried.

"Damnable!" some of them cursed.

"A perfect dragon!" swore others.

But the most furious were the sexton and the steward, both going almost mad with rage. The hostler was the only one who laughed.

"I'd sooner have guessed it was real Death stalking around as a ghost than Bára. She is a devilish woman!"

Miss Pepiňka just then burst into the company. The noise and confusion had attracted her from her room where she had already betaken herself to bed. She was wrapped in a shawl, on her head a yellow quilted nightcap. She always had to have something yellow on. She came with a lamp in one hand and an immense bundle of keys in the other. "For Heaven's sake, people, what has happened?" she cried, wholly terrified.

From several pairs of lips she heard the remarkable occurrence.

"BEWITCHED BÁRA"

"Oh, the godless, ungrateful girl!" exclaimed Pepinka in shocked amazement. "Just wait! She'll catch it from me! I'll read the gospel to her properly! Where have you got her?" she demanded.

"Who knows where she is? She disappeared in the middle of the bridge, just as if the earth had opened and swallowed her."

"Did she jump in the river?" questioned the priest.

"We heard no splash nor did we see anyone in the water. But then, reverend father, that is no trick for such a bewitched being! She can make herself invisible and is as much at home in fire as in water, up in the air as on earth, everywhere the same!" asserted one of the neighbors.

"Don't believe such nonsensical tales, my people!" the priest rebuked.

"Bára is a venturesome girl and has been carrying on mischief, but that is all, and for that she must be reprimanded. She must come to me to-morrow."

"Severely reprimanded, much respected sir!" exclaimed the steward, trembling with anger combined with the terror which had shaken his bones. "Very severely. It is a punishable offense to make a fool of the entire community."

"Oh, it wasn't as bad as that, precious sir," interrupted the peasants. "It was only the women who were frightened."

"My poor wife will have such a sick spell from the whole affair! It is unforgivable godlessness!" Vlček complained. Like the peasants, he did not mention his own fright.

Miss Pepinka was so rejoiced at the import of Vlček's speech that she could have forgiven Bára on the spot. But the hostler incensed her anew by saying: "Why should I deny it? I was really scared, though I'm not usually afraid of anything. We were all of us frightened. You, Mr. Sexton, could hardly crawl home, and the honorable Mr. Steward here was so terrified he dropped to his knees like an over-ripe pear. When she grinned her teeth at me I was sure it was Death itself—and it's no wonder, for I was three sheets in the wind. I expected her to clutch me by the throat, but instead she grabbed the steward here, lifted him up and screeched into his ears, 'If you ever dare show yourself again at the parsonage as a suitor you sign your own death-warrant.'"

The hostler wanted to demonstrate exactly how Bára seized the steward, but the latter dodged his grasp, his face changing from red to purple. But Miss Pepinka was terribly offended, although the peasants fully forgave Bára for putting them to the blush when they learned what she did to the steward. All further procedure was postponed till morning. The steward remained at the parsonage overnight, but by earliest dawn he was well on his way beyond the boundaries.

When in the morning Elška heard what Bára had ventured to do for her sake she begged her uncle and

Pepinka to forgive Bára, who had done it all to rid her of the steward. Miss Pepinka would not relinquish her plan and insisted that since Bára had so deeply affronted the steward she must be punished.

"And, moreover, if you don't marry the steward, you'll not get so much as a thread from me!" she threatened Elška, who only shrugged her shoulders.

The priest was not so stubborn. He did not wish to reprove his niece, but he could not wholly, of his own volition, forgive Bára. Elška was eager to go at once to Bára, but was not permitted to do so.

Jacob, knowing nothing of his daughter's secret doings, as usual took his horn the next morning and went out to call together his herd. But, to his amazement, nowhere were the gates opened—just as if during the night all the cattle had perished or as if the servants had overslept. He went up to the very houses and sounded his horn—loudly enough to call the dead from their graves. The cows bellowed, to be sure, but no one went to let them out. The maid-servants came out and said: "You are not to drive out our cows any more. Someone else is to do it!"

"What's that?" thought Jacob to himself, and went immediately to the mayor. Here he learned what had happened.

"We have nothing against you, personally, but your Bára is bewitched and the peasant women are afraid that she will cast a spell on them."

"Why, has anything ever happened to any of the herd?"

"No, but Bára might want to revenge herself."

"Leave my daughter alone!" cried Jacob angrily. "If you want my services, I'm willing to give them. If not, it's all right, too. The world is wide. God won't forsake us!"

"Well, you see, it wouldn't do to keep you, under the circumstances."

"Then put into your herdsman's hut whomsoever you please, and may you be here with God!" Jacob had never talked so much at once in all his life, nor had he ever been as angry as at that moment. He went home at once. Bára was not there. He went to untie Lišaj. The cow and bull which he had in charge were left to moo and bellow while he went to the parsonage.

Bára was standing before the priest.

"Did you parade around as a ghost?" the priest catechized her.

"Yes, reverend sir!" Bára answered dauntlessly.

"And why?"

"I knew the steward was a coward. I wanted to frighten him off so he wouldn't torture Miss Elška. She can't bear him and would die if she had to marry him."

"Remember its not your business to extinguish a fire that isn't burning you. Even without you, it would have been settled. How were you able to vanish so suddenly from the bridge?"

"Very easily, reverend sir. I cast off the sheets and

dress, jumped into the river and swam under water a short distance. That's why no one could see me."

"You swam under water?" The priest struck his hands together amazedly. "What a girl you are! And at night, too! Who taught you?"

Bára was amazed at the priest's surprise.

"Why, reverend sir, my father instructed me how I must move when in the water, and the rest I learned myself. That's no trick. I know every stone in the river. Why should I be afraid?"

The priest gave long-drawn-out admonitions to Bára and then sent her to the servants' hall to await judgment. He took consultation with the mayor, aldermen and the schoolmaster, and they decided that since Bára had caused such a general scandal and had been so audacious she must be publicly chastised. As a punishment they condemned her to remain shut up for one whole night in the vault at the cemetery. It seemed to all a terrible punishment, but since she had been so bold and unabashed, let her learn, they said, what real terror is by a night spent among dead men's bones.

Miss Pepinka was not at all pleased with the sentence. Elška was utterly shocked and every woman in the village shuddered with horror over the penalty imposed. Even the sexton's wife was willing to forgive Bára, and thought she would be sufficiently punished by the simple publication of the fact that judgment had been passed on her.

Bára, alone, remained unmoved. It worried her far more that the community had dismissed her father, for she had already heard what had happened to him. When the priest told her where she was to spend the succeeding night, she listened to all quietly, then kissed his hand, saying, "As far as that's concerned, it makes little difference if I sleep in the charnel-house or some other place. I can sleep even on a stone. But it's harder for father. What will become of him, now that they've taken his position away from him? Father can't live without his flocks and herds, for he's been used to them all his life. He will die! Arrange it somehow, reverend sir!"

Everyone marvelled at Bára's unsubdued spirit and refused to believe otherwise than that, after all, it was some sort of supernatural power that made Bára different from other people.

"Never mind, her crest will fall by night," many of them thought. But they were mistaken. Bára was dejected only until she learned that the peasants had returned to Jacob his work as public herdsman, which the priest had arranged for by giving him his own herd to pasture.

After dinner, when the priest was napping and Miss Pepinka was also dozing a little, Elška stole out from the room and ran down to Bára. Her eyes were red with weeping and she was shaking with fear. Violently she threw her arms around Bára's neck and fell to sobbing anew.

"BEWITCHED BÁRA" 211

"There, there, be quiet!" Bára consoled her. "Don't worry! Just let's be content if that cricket doesn't come courting you again, and he'd have to be a man without any sense of honor at all if he'd dare come another time. The rest will right itself!"

"But you, poor dear, to have to spend the night in the charnel-house. Dear Lord, I'll not have a moment's peace!"

"Don't have any anxiety on that score. I have slept near the cemetery more than once, and day and night it is before my eyes. Just you go to bed and to sleep! And please send word to father not to have any fears for me and to tie up Lišaj for the night so he won't follow me. Then tomorrow I'll tell you the whole affair and what a scare I gave the steward. You'll have a good laugh over it. And soon you'll get word from Mr. Hynek. But when you get away from this place, Elška, you'll surely not leave me here, will you?" Bára asked sadly.

Elška only pressed her hand, whispering, "You and I belong to each other!" Softly she slipped away. Bára sang cheerfully to herself and felt a great peace.

When it had become quite dark the sexton and the night watchman came to lead Bára away to the cemetery. Miss Pepinka winked at her to plead with the priest, intending herself to intercede also. But Bára would not understand, and when the priest himself said that if she asked mercy and was penitent those who had passed the decree could be prevailed upon she tossed her head defiantly, saying, "Since you were pleased to judge me deserving of punishment, I will serve out my sentence!" And she went with the men.

The people ran out of the houses, many of them feeling sorry for her, but Bára took no notice of any of them and walked merrily towards the graveyard, which was situated near the heel of the forest not far from the community pasture.

Her two escorts opened the door of the death-chamber where human bones and funeral biers were kept and, after expressing the wish, "May God protect you!" they went home.

From the vault a little window not much bigger than one's hand looked out on the valley and the forest. Bára stationed herself beside the window and looked out for a long, long time. Sad, indeed, must have been the thoughts that flitted through her mind, for tear after tear fell from her beautiful eyes and ran down her brown cheeks.

The moon rose higher and higher, one light after another in the village was extinguished, and more and more quiet it grew all around her. Over the graves fell the shadows of the tall pines standing near the wall and above the valley a light mist gathered. Only the barking or weird howling of dogs disturbed the stillness of the night.

Bára looked out upon the grave of her mother, recalled her lonely childhood, the dislike and scorn of

"BEWITCHED BÁRA" 213

her by the people of the village, and for the first time she felt the weight of it all and for the first time the thought came to her, "Oh, mother, would that I could be lying there beside you!" One thought gave birth to another, vision succeeded vision. In spirit she embraced the beautiful Elška, and on the forest path her imagination portrayed as by magic the figure of a tall, broad-shouldered huntsman, with a face expressing earnestness, energy and strength.

But finally she turned away from the window, shook her head silently and, covering her face with her hands, sank with a deep sigh to the ground, weeping and praying. Her deep sorrow allayed somewhat, she rose from the ground, intending to lie down on the funeral bier, when suddenly near the window a dog barked and a deep voice asked, "Bára, are you sleeping?" It was Jacob and Lišaj.

"I'm not sleeping, father, but I soon shall be. Why did you come? I'm not afraid."

"All right then, girl, sleep. I will sleep out here— it's a warm night." And her father lay down beneath the window, with Lišaj beside him.

They slept well until morning.

In the morning when the first streaks of dawn began to show, a man dressed in huntsman's costume came through the forest. Jacob often used to see him going through the forest or the valley.

"What are you doing here, Jacob?" the huntsman asked him as he drew near.

"Well, sir, they locked my daughter in here overnight and so I couldn't stand it to stay at home."

"Bára? What has happened?" the huntsman asked in amazement.

Jacob related all briefly. The huntsman uttered an oath, and then jerking the gun from his shoulder, hung it on a tree and nimbly scaled the cemetery wall. With a swing of his powerful right arm he forced open the door of the charnel-house and stood before Bára, whom the noise had awakened. Seeing the huntsman before her, she was under the impression that she was still dreaming, but hearing his voice, she wondered how he had come there and could not in her embarrassment even thank him for his greeting.

"Don't be angry, Bára, because I have burst in here this way. I was going past, saw your father and heard from him what had occurred to place you here, and it made me furious. Come away at once from these dead things!" the huntsman urged, taking Bára by the hand.

"Not yet, sir. I shall stay here until they come for me. They would say that I ran away. I really wasn't so uncomfortable here," Bára demurred lightly, withdrawing her hand from the grasp of the huntsman.

"Then I shall call your father and we shall both stay here," said the huntsman and shouted over the wall to Jacob.

So Jacob, too, climbed over the stone enclosure. Together they entered into the death-chamber to join

"BEWITCHED BÁRA" 215

Bára. Lišaj, who had bounded after Jacob, did not know what to do for joy when he saw Bára again.

When Jacob saw where Bára had slept he was almost ready to burst into sobs, and so to cover up his tears he went to the grave of his dead wife. The huntsman sat down on the bier. Bára played with Lišaj, but all the while she was conscious that the huntsman never took his eyes from her. She blushed and then paled and her heart pounded more violently than it had throughout the night when she had been wholly alone in the tomb.

"And is there no one beside your father in the entire village who would have looked after you here?" the huntsman asked after a while.

"Besides Elška and my father there is no one. Father came. Elška cannot come, and there is no one else who loves me that much. Excepting you, Lišaj, isn't that so?" And she gazed into the eyes of her dog. "And then everyone's afraid to go near the cemetery at night," she added.

"I marvel at your courage as I marvelled at your strength. Almost every day I have told my mother about you," said the huntsman.

"Oh, you still have a mother, sir?" Bára asked in gentle tones.

"Yes, an aged mother. We live together high up on the hill three-quarters of an hour's distance from here, in the forest. I am a huntsman. My mother has wished for a daughter and would like to see me happy. I have never found anywhere a woman I would want for a wife until I saw you. Bára, I am not a man of long speeches. I have cared for you from the moment I first saw you. I've learned to know you well, too, even though we did not talk to each other, and that I have said nothing before this is because I did not dare presume to ask your consent. Now you know all. Tell me if you think you can care for me—and if you want to be my wife. In Vestec you cannot remain after this. So if you care for me, take what things you wish with you and come at once with your father to me up there to our home in the forest where people will love you."

Bára stood like a statue, not moving a muscle, nor could she utter a single word. The huntsman did not know how to interpret this but, wishing to learn the truth, even if it should prove bitter for him, he again asked Bára if she would become his wife. Then the girl burst into tears and cried out: "Dear God! Is it really true that you love me?" The huntsman assured her with his lips and the warm clasp of his hand, and only then did she avow her long-cherished love for him.

Having come to a happy understanding, they emerged and knelt before Jacob. The huntsman said: "You know me, father, and you know that for a long time now I have been amply able to support a wife. But none pleased until I saw your daughter. I fell in love with her that very first time. She and I have just come to an agreement, and we want your blessing.

"BEWITCHED BÁRA" 217

Even though we are in a cemetery, this, too, is God's domain—God Himself is everywhere!"

Jacob did not ask any long-drawn-out questions, only assuring himself that Bára herself was contented. He gave them his blessing and then the three made further plans and arrangements.

How astonished the sexton was when, after ringing the morning bell for early prayers, he came for Bára and found her in the company of her father and her accepted suitor, as the huntsman immediately announced himself to be.

There was even greater amazement at the parsonage and in the entire village. The people had thought Bára would be tamed down, the Lord only knows how much, and how humble she would be—and now she was returning as the betrothed of such a splendid man. They could not even believe it to be possible that "bewitched Bára" could win anyone's love—but it had come to pass.

"She has luck from hell itself," the girls in the village told each other.

But sincere and great was the rejoicing of Elška when Bára brought her lover to her friend.

"See, God has repaid the service that you rendered me and for which you suffered so much. I knew that you would find a man who would truly love you. You must love her deeply—for she deserves it most fully," the good girl said, turning to the huntsman and extending her hand, which he clasped earnestly.

The huntsman wished very much to take Bára with him at once, but things did not move as rapidly as that, as Miss Pepinka would not consent to let Bára go before the formal wedding. Better to have all three publications of the banns of marriage at once when the bridegroom is impatient. Jacob, too, could not at once tear himself from the herdsman's cottage.

Bára grieved most deeply about Elška. But the next day a letter arrived from Prague for the priest, in which the aunt stated that she would bequeath all her wealth to her niece on the single condition that she marry the young doctor who had cured her (the aunt) and that the priest should ask Elška to decide yes or no on the matter. When also a special letter was enclosed for Elška full of the most beautiful hopes for an early meeting, then Bára had no more unfulfilled desires.

Before the wedding all the people of the village became reconciled with Bára. Even the sexton's wife wished her happiness and handed her a letter from Josífek. Elška read it to Bára and then only did the latter learn what Elška had long known, that Josífek loved her and only on Bára's account had not wanted to become a priest. But since she was to marry another he would now accede to his parents' wishes and enter the priesthood.

A week later Miss Pepinka prepared a fine wedding for Bára. The huntsman's dear old mother came also to take away with her the daughter to whose coming

"BEWITCHED BÁRA"

she had looked forward for a long time. Jacob went with them.

When the huntsman was leading his young wife through the house he brought her to the room which had been his own. From the wall above the bed he took down a wreath which was now all withered.

"Do you recognize it?" he asked Bára. It was the very wreath which had caught on the branches of the willow on St. John's morn. Bára smiled.

"Whom were you thinking of when you threw it to the water?" questioned the huntsman, drawing her to his heart.

Bára did not answer, but put her arms around his neck and lifted up to him a pair of lovely, smiling eyes which the people had called "bull's eyes," but which the huntsman regarded as the most beautiful eyes in the whole wide world.

ALOIS JIRÁSEK

(Born August 23, 1851, in Hronov.)

ALOIS JIRÁSEK was born of a family of small farmers and weavers of modest means. In his native district near Náchod, the bloodiest scenes of the Prussian war of 1866 took place and on young Jirásek that period of his country's history left an ineffaceable effect. The wars in which his people fell, from earliest times to his own day, whether in a cause they themselves upheld or to gain the selfish ends of the monarch who controlled the man power of the nation, form the basis of most of his elaborate historical novels as well as of many of his shorter tales.

While an instructor in the college at Litomyšl, where he remained some eighteen years, he gathered further material for novels whose background shows his intimate knowledge of the history and traditions of that locality rich in the lore he sought. His student novels "Filosofská Historie" (A Philosopher's Story) on which he later based his drama "M. D. Rettigová," together with all the stories included in his "Máloměstské Historie" (Small Town Stories), his three-part novel "F. L. Věk" concerned with the torchbearers of literary, linguistic and political progress, his drama

"Vojnárka" based on the later religious struggle of the Čzechs, the sharply cut figures in his play of "Otec" all owe their origin to the influence of the Litomyšl district.

Jirásek excels as a novelist in using the times of John Huss and the Hussite Wars as a background and in merging himself deep in the significance of that period for his nation and for the world in general. The first fruits of his study of the spiritual revolution in Bohemia was his romance, "Slavný Den" (The Glorious Day) in the collection entitled "In Stormy Days." The crest of the Hussite period is described in "Proti Všem" (Against All) which had been prepared for in the "Mezi Proudy" (Between Currents), and these two books with "Bratrstvo" (Brotherhood) complete a wonderful trilogy. In the final work "Bratrstvo," Jirásek rises to his best as a painter of far-reaching struggles and great national enthusiasms. Here Henryk Sienkiewicz in no wise excels the Czech artist.

In "V Cizích Službách" (In Foreign Service) Jirásek gives a close but heartbreaking view of the part played by a chivalrous Czech in the defense of a Bavarian ruler—another tragic parallel to the "Anabasis."

His short stories, like his more extensive pieces of work, are concerned with three main themes: first the splendor of the non-producing class—the nobility— contrasted with the squalor and sorrow of the workers, second, the careers of the soldiers of his native land in home and foreign fields, and third, the life of the people of his native district during the period of the nation's downfall. His best known collections are the "Small Town Tales," "In Stormy Days," "Short Stories and Sketches," "Homeward and Other Sketches," and "From Diverse Ages." A very popular collection of legends of local Czech origin is his "Staré Pověsti České" (Old Czech Legends) published in 1894 and later issued in several editions. Another favorite collection for younger readers is his "From Bohemia to the End of the World." Alois Jirásek has been the recipient of many honors from his countrymen in recent times, in recognition of his many and great contributions to literature and of his work in building up through his stalwart patriotism and opposition to lukewarmness and hypocrisy a sturdy uncompromising spirit in matters pertaining to the national welfare.

THE PHILOSOPHERS

BY ALOIS JIRÁSEK

THE old entrenchment of a field battery near the small wood, now half sunken and overgrown with shrubbery, has stood in the solitude of the fields for a good hundred years. It alone has remained of all the fortifications and mounds which extended here in a long line through the plain, concealing numberless Prussian cannon aimed against the emperor's army protected by trenches. Now it resembles an ancient tomb in which herdsmen, on misty mornings or cold evenings, build fires to warm themselves and from which they halloo into the distance.

In the year 1778 during the war over the Bavarian succession, all the country along the Medhuj and the upper Elbe, containing two armies, resembled an immense anthill. At the head of the Prussian army, Friedrich; against him, Joseph, both philosophers.

A heavy fog had settled on the country like a deep lake. It was early in the morning, quiet and soundless, as if not a soldier were near. Nowhere was ringing of bells permitted, but instead there sounded, in a man's voice, the old song "Whoever the protection of the Highest—"

Václav Suk, soldier of the emperor's regiment under Hiller, standing far out in the front guard on the edge of the grassy dale, heard that song. Thick underbrush concealed half his body. Because it was cold he had rolled his gray cape closely up to his three-cornered hat so that not even his braided cue was visible. And now came that song—as if from directly opposite him! Was the enemy so close? How could it be?

Suk liked best a worldly song with his comrades beside the fire or before the booth of some youthful female cantinière, but this time the religious song moved him strangely. His grandmother used to sing it from parlor to bedroom and from chamber to garret, when her loose slippers, pattering, woke the whole household.

Suk took up the song also. The voice opposite ceased for a moment, then sounded anew and the old song was carried on the waves of the gradually lifting fog.

Václav, however, could not stand it long. His curiosity got the better of him. The unknown on the other side of the hollow sang on like a music master and it seemed as if he wished to finish out the stanzas just as Suk's grandmother used to do.

"Say, you, over there, are you a soldier?"

That is how Suk began the conversation and he did not speak into unanswering mist. He learned that he was talking with a soldier of the Prussian advance guard.

THE PHILOSOPHERS

"And how is it that you are a Brandenburger and yet speak the Czech language?"

"I am a Czech of Kladsko on the Bohemian borders. I am serving in the army, by God's will, my second year now—."

"He is a pious man," thought Suk to himself. "Without a doubt he is of the Helvetian confession," and he expressed this conjecture aloud. The Prussian confirmed the surmise.

"And what is your name?"

"Jan Koláčný."

"And here we are talking—what would our masters say to us?"

"Why, are we doing something wicked?"

"To be sure, we are fellow countrymen, both Czechs. When will such a meeting as this occur again?"

The conversation lagged. Suk saw through the mist which was gradually growing lighter the silhouette of the Prussian soldier in his spiked cap resembling a bishop's mitre. He was standing beside an old thickly crowned bushy beech. After a pause, Suk began, "It's very cold to-day—."

"It is. Come here and get warm." Koláčný urged as genuinely as if he stood on the threshold of his snow-covered mountain cottage.

"Where?"

"Here to me. I have a full bottle—."

Suk stood rigid. Suspicion was awakened. Some

trick perhaps—and then—to go away from the spot appointed to him as guard! Koláčný understood.

"Fear not, friend! How could I injure you? Let us lay aside our weapons and each go half way." That voice did not deceive and Suk saw that Koláčný was propping his gun against a tree trunk. He looked around and went forward. Half way forward the soldiers met. The Prussian enemy with undisguised sincerity extended his hand.

"Just come, don't be afraid. You and I have done nothing wrong to each other. We are brothers of one blood. What matters it to us what the rulers of these lands have done to each other?" said the Helvetian bible-loving descendant of the exiled Bohemian brethren emigrants. And the lively lad from the home kingdom understood him.

As these two deliberated, so, surely, many before them had reflected and doubtless many in future shall do, whether kings be philosophers or, as Plato dreamed —philosophers be kings.

"And here it ended," added the old schoolmaster, who related the incident to me, as it had been handed down from ancient chronicles, indicating the ruined earthworks in which we paused to rest. "Both of the wise men became engrossed in conversation and were caught at it. Here in this place sat the Prussian king and hither they brought Koláčný for trial. He told all and in a short while after, they shot him down over there behind the breastworks. The other one

THE PHILOSOPHERS 229

escaped lead and powder, to be sure. But he ran a bloody gauntlet and God knows where he completed the rest of his punishment."

And there you have it—what is there to an army that philosophizes and reflects?

IGNÁT HERRMAN

(Born August 12, 1854, in Chotěboř.)

HERRMAN worked himself up from a lowly grocer apprenticeship through the gradations of lawyer's copyist, commercial traveler, business manager, court reporter to the position of editor of a prominent Prague newspaper. In each of these spheres he had ample opportunity to study the life of Prague, and it is in his faithful presentation of figures in the Bohemian capital that he is at his best. While he draws faithfully —even to their slang—the rougher quarters of the city, he is an artist and not a mere photographer or phonograph record. His short stories of character and incident breathe an underlying understanding of human nature and the sympathy of a true member of the brotherhood of man. In all his works, the touch of quiet humor which his public always enjoyed, for it is seldom tinged with sarcasm, was never lacking. Oddly enough, his only somber work, "U Snědeného Krámu" (The Ruined Shop), detailing the downfall of a Prague shop-keeping family, is adjudged to be his best, though two humorous novels, "Otec Kondelík a Ženich Vejvara" (Father Kondelík and Suitor Vejvara" and its sequel "Tchán Kondelík a Zeť Vejvara"

(Father-in-law Kondelík and Son-in-law Vejvara) went through several editions. His collections of short stories which are most widely read are "Pražské Figurky" (Prague Types); "Drobní Lidé" (Insignificant People); "Z Pražských Zákoutí" (From Prague Nooks) and "Bodří Pražané" (Gay Praguers).

The story selected is from his "Drobní Lidé" and was written in 1885. The title refers to an actual author, Madame Rettigová, who published several novels and also a practical "Domácí Kuchařka" (Home Cook-Book).

WHAT IS OMITTED FROM THE COOK-BOOK OF MADAME MAGDÁLENA DOBROMILA RETTIGOVÁ

A CHRISTMAS GLEANING

BY IGNÁT HERRMAN

"Why are you all the time fussing in those shelves?" howled out the chief counsellor at Konopásek, the day-clerk who alone of the force remained in the office on Christmas day.

It was late in the afternoon. The attorney was hastily completing some documents in order not to have so much to do after the holidays and was angry at the clerk, who had already arisen several times from his copying work and had been rooting around in the cabinet where the supplies were kept. First, he needed writing-sand, next he looked for a longer ruler, again he picked around among pieces of sealing wax. Up to this moment the counsellor had said nothing and had only pulled at his nose, as was his habit when inward wrath overpowered him—but finally the constant running about of the lean, gray-haired clerk exasperated him to such a pitch that he burst out on him.

"It's nothing, Mr. Counsellor, nothing," answered

Konopásek quickly and his ashen cheeks reddened with a faint flush. "I just ran out of twine and I'd like to sew up that inventory. I'm just going for a fresh ball—"

"Zounds, man! Don't you see right there on the table before you a ball as big as thunder?" howled the counsellor angrily and pointed to a ball of black and yellow twine lying right in front of Konopásek's nose, so to speak.

"You're so excited about your Christmas dinner of fried carp that you're absolutely stupid, it seems to me. It'll not run away."

Konopásek with red cheeks sat down at his place and sewed on. After a while, however, he rose again, stepped quickly to the door, took the key from the wainscot and hastily walked out of the office.

When he had left, the attorney arose as if something had pierced him and with short steps approached the cabinet. He opened it and looked at the supplies in which Konopásek had been rummaging. There was almost nothing inside. Some paper, a bit of string, a few sticks of sealing wax and two pairs of scissors. In a corner of the compartment were several small circular boxes on the lid of each of which was pasted a round white wafer, about the size of a cent, a hardened thin disk of flour or gelatin used for sealing official documents. One of the boxes stood at a little distance from the others. The counsellor involuntarily took hold of it to push it closer to the others, but suddenly lifted it.

A CHRISTMAS GLEANING 235

It was suspiciously light—empty. The counsellor raised a second box, shook it—it was empty. He took a third, fourth, fifth—all were empty and only the last two were filled with the round, white wafers. The counsellor pushed his spectacles up on his forehead. What did this mean? . . . Why, he himself had bought a supply only two weeks ago—on what things could they all have been pasted in so short a time? He was still standing beside the cabinet when Konopásek re-entered the office. Observing the attorney beside the cabinet, he turned as white as the wall.

"Well, where did you put all the wafers? Speak up!"

"Oh, Mr. Counsellor!" cried out the pale, trembling clerk, clasping his hands imploringly. "Do not destroy me—I have a wife and six children!"

Until that moment the counsellor had not a thought of anything irregular, but now he suspected something was wrong, yet he could not grasp what it might be. The wafers—what had happened?

The crushed, deadly pale, shivering clerk reached with his bony fingers into the tail of his shabby, greenish-colored coat and drew therefrom a pocket-handkerchief, filled up, the corners being drawn together and tied.

"Here they are—every one of them," he stammered with chattering teeth. "I will put them all back into the boxes." He untied the corners of the handkerchief and poured out on a sheet of paper a small pile of wafers.

Now at last the attorney comprehended that the clerk had taken them, but why—for what possible purpose? And curiosity overpowering his obligatory official wrath, the counsellor impatiently exploded.

"What did you intend to do with them, Konopásek?"

"Supper—an evening meal, your honor!" stuttered Konopásek. "It is Christmas day. I haven't even a sixpence. I promised my wife I'd bring some wafers—she wanted to bake them with shreds of fat. I have six children and I must make some sort of Christmas for them. They haven't eaten all day—there was nothing in the house—."

The counsellor slid the spectacles down from his forehead to his eyes, gazed at the pile of white, tasteless, unsalted, starchy wafers and then he meant to look at Konopásek, but suddenly his glance shifted from the miserable, twitching face with its blue lips on which trembled the gray streaked moustache and fixing his eyes on the clerk's faded, stained necktie, he asked, "Have you ever eaten them before, Konopásek?"

"Yes, sir," uttered the quivering lips of the clerk.

"Is the stuff really eatable?" asked the amazed attorney.

"Indeed, yes, Mr. Counsellor. Dear Lord, if one only had enough of them—."

"Put them back into the boxes!" commanded the counsellor in a voice bristling suddenly as he turned to his own desk.

The clerk raked the wafers with his thin, ink-spotted

A CHRISTMAS GLEANING

fingers and filled the emptied boxes. When he had finished this, he sat down on a chair to continue his work. But he could not go on. His fingers trembled, in his eyes a mist formed and there was a roaring in his temples. Shame, dismissal, wretchedness—and after all, the children will have nothing to eat to-day!

The attorney glanced at Konopásek several times and wiped his glasses and his eyes, after which he sneezed violently a number of times. He, too, could not work. He was doubtless angry at the good-for-nothing clerk who stole wafers in order to bake them up with shreds of fat, for a Christmas dinner for his children. He twisted for a while in his chair, rose finally and approached the door. The clerk shivered anew. Now he was to hear his fate.

The attorney stepped a little closer to the transgressor, and not looking at Konopásek, ordered, "Take your coat and hat and go to the market. Buy a carp, a good big one and take it home to the wife at once, you understand? So that she'd have time to get it ready. Then buy the children nuts and apples and for your wife get a bottle of punch or tea or whatever you want to drink after supper. Here, take this and get out!"

At the concluding words, he drew from his pocket a wallet, opened it, took out a bit of paper and laid it on the table. The astonished Konopásek saw before him a ten-florin note.

"Jesus Mary, Mr. Counsellor!" broke from the lips

of Konopásek. But further words he was unable to utter. Perhaps, because the attorney made a violent gesture of protest or more likely, because the poor clerk's whole face and body quivered as with chills and fever. He was choked with amazement, surprise, joy—all!

In an instant after, the counsellor remained alone in the office, but he had no more inclination to work. He arose after a while, put on his handsome fur cloak, thrust his hands into his shaggy modern woolly mittens and, closing the office, departed. He walked lightly, joyously—and thought of his own six children looking forward to the delight they would have over the gifts which for many weeks were being collected in a rear room. But at times a sort of dejection and melancholy oppressed him. That was whenever his thoughts involuntarily reverted to Konopásek and his "wafers with shreds of fat," as the clerk had described the dish.

JAN KLECANDA

(Born March 5, 1855, in Prague.)

AMONG the newspaper men of Bohemia who have become prolific story writers is Jan Klecanda, who for a long period of years has been in the service of the Czech minority in the northern part of Bohemia where the German population has steadily increased through systematic efforts to dispossess the native Czechs.

He is a productive writer who has to his credit twenty-one volumes of novels, sketches and short stories chiefly depicting life among the laboring classes and the nationalistic struggles of the Czechs against the Teutons in the territory adjacent to the northern boundary.

Mr. Klecanda has had the opportunity of observing acutely the methods of Germanization practiced in the borderland of his own country, which was systematically invaded by those who sowed propaganda through the agency of industrial enterprises on purchased lands. Often he saw children alienated from their parents and taught to scorn their native tongue by the enforced substitution in the north Bohemian districts of the German for the Czech language. The accompanying story "For the Land of His Fathers" (Za Půdu Otců) is taken from the collection entitled "Tvrdé Hlavy" (Stubborn Heads), which has enjoyed much popularity.

Other collections of stories ranging from tragedy and pathos to gentlest humor are: "Mezi Víry a Skalisky" (Among Whirlpools and Cliffs); "Hrdinové Malých Románů" (Heroes of Small Romances); "Vojáci v Miru" (Warriors of Peace); "Na Bojišti" (On the Battle Field), the last two of which went through several editions.

FOR THE LAND OF HIS FATHERS

BY JAN KLECANDA

I

"FATHER!" sounded the voice of the young master of the estate from the courtyard.

"Well, what is it?" responded his old father with an ill-humored question which expressed no pleasant anticipation of what the "young master" would have to say.

"Oh, well, nothing! I just thought I'd mention a certain matter so you'd not be too frightened when the gentlemen come to-morrow," the younger man said somewhat irresolutely, and throwing away the ax with which he had been splitting wood, he straightened up from his work as if preparing to ward off an attack.

"What's that?—'gentlemen' to see us? What kind of 'gentlemen'? From the courts? For the execution of a mortgage?" the questions fairly rushed from the fear tightened throat of the old man, who, though in his sixties, was still stalwart.

"Why, what are you thinking of?" the young man waved his hand, rather glad that his father had immediately suspected something evil and that, therefore, his report would affect him the less. "The German gentlemen from the factory will come here to inspect the place."

"And what have they to inspect here? Has something been lost from the factory and has suspicion fallen on you?" The words were as if ejected from the lips of the old man as he leaped close to the fence on which he leaned the better to look closely into his son's eyes.

"What wild guesses you are making to-day. Am I a ruffian or thief to have that sort of visitations? And if they did have it in for me, they surely wouldn't announce their visit beforehand.'

"Of course, of course!" assented the old man. "Such a visit, though, is as rare as if it fell from heaven, even though the devil may bring them. You don't have an idea where or why,—and a gendarme lands before you with handcuffs, and the mayor—but God save us from that!"

"There, there! Don't worry about the gentlemen from the courts and their helpers!"

"Well, then, tell what's happened and don't torture me! It won't be anything pleasant, I'm sure, for these German "gentlemen" never cross the threshold of a poor man to bring him anything good!"

"Well—you'll see! You yourself say, 'There is no rule without an exception,' and this time it's proven true. Money is something good, isn't it?"

"Money? I should say so!" assented the old man, delighted, but in the next instant he burst out with another doubt. "But why should the gentlemen run after you?"

"Oh, that's all a part of it!" the young man drew himself up boastfully. "Only that they won't run, but will come in style in a carriage and then I will ride away with them!"

"You will ride?—That's getting better all the time, boy! When our rich men give one a ride, then it's sure to end well! Well, hurry up and speak!"

"Speak, speak! But you don't let a man get in a word. Well, then listen. I've made an agreement with the gentleman that I'll sell him this hut." The young man spoke rapidly as if to have the confession out.

"What? What's that you said, in God's name?" shrieked the old man and leaped up as if a hornet had stung him.

"Well—now—I'm speaking Czech and loud enough, too," growled the son peevishly, angered by his father's terror, which augured nothing good.

"But still I did not understand you, Joseph! Say it again, I beg of you," pleaded the older man in an appeasing tone.

"Well, I was saying that I'm going to sell the homestead to the gentleman. He needs a place for a building. He needs the garden and also the field beyond it."

"Needs? Needs? And what is it to you that he needs it?" the old man echoed in a threatening voice, and it seemed as if his figure, standing erect on the other side of the fence, had grown in height.

"Well, you needn't yell at me as if I were a mere boy, or half the village will come running here," the son said soothingly. "It's nothing to me what he needs, but it is something to me that he is offering a thousand more than the place is really worth, and a thousand extra is mighty good money these days."

The old man did not speak at once, but pushed his shaggy cap back on his head and with his calloused hand wiped off the sweat which had burst out on his forehead. Then he stepped to the gate which he pushed open with his foot and entered the yard. He stalked towards his son with energetic strides and grasped his stick firmly as if he intended to use it.

Pausing before his son, in deep yet sharp tones he uttered, "A thousand—you are right—is good money, providing it is honest profit!"

"And isn't this honest, when I sell what is mine?" the young man defended himself rebelliously, irritated by his father's opposition.

The old man vainly gasped for breath enough to answer. His face turned red, then paled and purpled with emotion and wrath. Joseph saw his father's struggle, but in order to avoid looking at him, he turned away, picked up his ax and started at his work again.

"Leave that alone, now, Joseph! It won't run away!" the old man forced himself to be gentle when he could again regain his speech. "Let's go into the house and talk it over."

His son, however, frowned, but still did not dare raise any objection. He threw the ax away, kicked fiercely at the pile of wood until it scattered in all directions and then followed his father, muttering in vexation, "A man has to go into a conference just when he has so much to do that he doesn't know what to leap at first."

The father, acting as if he did not see his son's anger, went to the house, opened the door and stooping, entered. The young man followed but he did not need to stoop to enter.

When they had stepped inside, the old man threw his cap on the table behind which he seated himself on the bench near the wall. The young man remained standing near the door, crushing his cap in his hands in sullen indecision.

"Well, come on and sit down, Joseph," the old man urged in the most agreeable tones he could force from his throat. "You are the master here and it is not fitting that you should stand at the door like some passing vagabond!"

"So there! I'm the master, am I?" said the son in cutting tones, and approaching the table, sat down sprawlingly on the chair. He gazed at his father in a challenging manner as if he wished to frighten him and give himself more courage.

"Master, to be sure!" repeated the old man.

"Haven't I always shown respect for you as the master of the place, even though you are the son and I the father? You are master of all here except of my little reserve plot,"[1] he uttered the last words with distinct emphasis as if he were treading on a loud pedal for each syllable, "and what you command, shall be done. May it all be worthy!"

"And don't I look after the homestead as well as can be done? Haven't I grubbed out of this dry soil every bit that it possibly could be lashed into giving? And won't I give you all that is written down in the contract?" the son struck out at his father.

"Don't scold me that way. I don't want any quarrels. I say, not an egg nor a liter of milk have you or Apolena cheated me out of.—May God repay her for it! And you labor and save—all honor to you both!" gravely spoke the aged man.

"Well, then what's the matter?" violently hurled back the son, adding quickly, "And all this toiling— what's it all for? You can't make a living on it. It will sooner raise thorns and weeds than grain enough for a loaf of bread, without even speaking of koláče. So, what to do with it?"

"May God not punish you for those hard words," cried the father in deep grief. "Honestly has this

---

[1] The word is "výměnek," signifying a small cottage with enough attached land or a sum set aside to provide maintenance for a parent who has bequeathed all his property to the children and has retired from its active management. It is a custom among the Czechs and Slovaks to reserve a plot of ground or a pension for their old age.

soil supported us and before us our grandfather and before him all our forefathers. From time out of mind the Nešněras have occupied this land and have provided dowers for their daughters and portions for the sons, as well as has anyone else and yet there was always bread enough remaining for all. And you are not able to make a living here when you had no debts to pay and are the only child?"

"Make a living or not—that isn't the question! I don't want to. I've had enough of plodding over these clods. And why shouldn't I sell when he wants it and will pay well for it?"

"Dear Christ Jesus!" sighed the old man. "When you talk this way and only chatter of money, we never will get to an agreement."

"So you see, father, it's best not to talk at all. You know I've inherited a head as stubborn as yours and what gets sown in it, you can't thresh out with a club," the son reminded him almost gently.

But that gentleness which was forced and artificial was like oil poured on a fire. The old man leaped up, and swinging his heavy cane over his head, screamed, "If I knew it would help, if it's to be a question of your head or my stick, I'd—."

The door creaked and the son's wife with their two boys entered. The old man, seeing his daughter-in-law with the children, quickly laid his stick on the table. He honored in his son the father of a family and did not wish to cause unpleasantness for the children.

"What are you coming here for? Who called you in?" the young man burst out angrily at his wife.

"We surely belong here without being called in, don't we? And your wife can hear what you have to say to your father?" the mistress of the home calmly answered.

"Right you are, Apolena. Just come here and let me hear what you think of this. And you boys also. It's a matter that concerns your inheritance!"

The master irritably crushed his cap down on his head and arose, intending to leave.

"Stay here, Joseph," said the old man mildly, yet with a tone of firm command, "when I honor the father in you, you too, must honor the grandfather in the presence of my grandchildren. And after all, it's the concern of the entire family. This land, in the name of our Christ Jesus, does not belong to you alone, but to all the Nešněras who, God granting, will yet succeed us!"

"Oh, then talk as much as you please, but I say it's all useless," said the master and carelessly and with an air of resignation he sat down again.

"Well, then, what do you say to it, Apolena?" the old man turned to his daughter-in-law, his voice shaken by emotion. "Or didn't you know, either, that Joseph intends to sell this 'hut'—as he called it to-day— to that German?"

"In God's name, father!" burst forth the young woman and tears suddenly filled her eyes. "I have implored him on my knees and with clasped hands. I've said, 'Joseph, day and night until my limbs give way under me will I toil if only you will not drive us out of here.' But all pleading is in vain. Sooner could you squeeze a tear out of a rock!"

"So much has he hardened against his own family!" bitterly complained the old man. "And for a miserable thousand he has—sold himself!"

"And we'll have an easier living! After all, I will stay on my own soil, for I'm to look after the place for the German master," the son defended himself in some embarrassment.

"On your own soil? That will be wholly different. Now you are master here, then you will be a master's servant or lackey! And you'll serve by the hour! When it suits him, he'll drive you out. And you'll leave the homestead to which cling the blood and sweat of your forefathers. So you wanted an easier living? And you seek it at a German's? My boy, we of the mountains are not born for, nor do we fit an easy life. What God gave, take, even though it be little—there will be enough. But from a German, it is as if you accepted water in a sieve!"

"But it's to be by written contract! Am I a child that I'm to be fooled by empty words? You've heard that I'm to go in a carriage with them to the notary and there it will all be properly recorded."

"What will be recorded there? Your shame for everlasting memory? Listen, Joseph,"—the old man spoke almost majestically, raising himself earnestly from the bench,—"your aged father, grown gray in honest toil, is speaking to you. I, too, might have had an easier living. Temptation came to me, also, but when I saw you growing up into such a fine, stalwart youth, I said to myself, 'No, the Nešněras must not die out here on this land of my fathers!' Look, you could cut into this palm of mine, so hardened it is by labor. And for whom? For you and yours! And why? Because this land is sacred to me, because I know how my father and grandfather toiled here. That was in the times when the overlord's feudal lash hissed over them. This piece of land, because it lay so close to the castle, always pierced the eyes of the nobles. They wanted to buy us out—drive us away from here. Much blood our fathers shed, but they did not yield a single span of the land.—And see, Joseph, it was only in that way that we have preserved our Czech nation by defending every inch of our native land in a tooth and nail struggle against our enemy! To-day the nation extols us. Yes, in a thousand years they will still bless us that we—simple peasants and cottagers devoting our lives lovingly to our soil—preserved the land untainted for our children!"

Wonderfully touching, yes, even terrible was the look on the grandfather's face as he stood there livid, the muscles of his face torn, his gray hair disarranged and pasting itself on his forehead with the perspiration that poured from him. The two boys looked in terror first at their grandfather, then at their father who sat defiantly with his gaze fastened on the floor.

Apolena wiping her tear-dimmed eyes on her sleeve, approached her husband and laying her hand on his shoulder, said in a voice of emotion thrilling with deep anxiety, "Father, husband — look! It is your own father! You will kill him thus! Is this the way to repay him for all his care, in his old age?"

"Don't I respect my father? And do I want to injure him? He, too, will be better off in a new place than now—"

"What? What's that you said?" screamed the father and with the agility of a youth he leaped in front of his son. "I am to be with you? In a new place? And do you think, Joseph, that you'd drive even me out of my own little reserve plot and that I, too, will let myself be bought? No, I thank God now, that I remembered to keep a little corner for myself though I never dreamed it might come to this!"

"Well, father, when we go, you go with us. A sale is a sale, and there all 'reserve rights' cease," said the son in a calmer voice.

"If you want to sell your land, sell it," responded the old man with cutting coldness. "Sell the roof over your head, sell your land on which you might have rested, sell all that your fathers and forefathers preserved for you for hundreds of years, but what is mine you shall not sell, do you understand?" and in the speech of the old man there sounded such a threat that

Joseph dropped his eyes and his wife shivered in sudden terror.

"Husband of mine, in the name of Christ Jesus," she moaned, twining her arms around his neck, "such a thing as this has never come between us!"

"And am I to blame for it? Why are you moaning and wailing here?" Joseph shouted as he pushed her away so roughly that she staggered.

There was no need to notice it, for Joseph in reality had not struck his wife. Old Nešněra might not have noticed it ordinarily, for he never meddled in their affairs. But to-day, Apolena was on his side and the deed offered a welcome opportunity for him to rebuke his son.

"So my son Joseph beats his wife because she takes the part of her father-in-law?" he shrieked. "Did you ever see me raise my hand against your mother?"

The young master feeling that in this instance a wrong was being done to him, for he had not even thought of striking his wife, jumped up, seized his cap, and rushed out of the room. Out in the yard, he paused, lifted his cap, and ran his hand over his brow as if wiping away the perspiration and then, spitting in disgust, walked out towards the highway.

In domestic quarrels, the sole consolation and refuge of the one who forsakes the battlefield is the tavern. And so Nešněra, too, directed his steps to the inn to drown the entire ugly occurrence in beer.

FOR THE LAND OF HIS FATHERS 253

At home, for a while after his departure, a painful silence reigned. The old man felt that he had wronged his son in his last speech and for that reason he was slightly shaken in his own stand, so firm heretofore. But Nešněra was too honest a man not to own frankly that he was at fault.

"You know, Apolenka," he said after a moment, "Joseph did not even intend to strike you. It was only an accident—"

"But he didn't even hurt me, father," eagerly the wife defended him. "He just swung his arm—"

"Well, then, praise be to God, that from that quarter the clouds are driven away," the old man rejoiced. "Now, if only we can chase the shadows away in the other matter. But you are with me in that and you will not permit the land which bore so many Nešněras to go into a stranger's hands. You see, Apolenka, you, too, are of peasant origin and though you were not born under this roof, you feel with me what it would mean to have our property fall into alien hands!"

II

"Well, what's up. Why are you rushing about with your eyes on top of your head, as if you were hunting a midwife?" so one of young Nešněra's friends at the inn greeted him while the others burst into merry laughter.

"Oh, nothing!" Joseph disposed of the inquisitive one peevishly. "Had a little squabble at home."

"With whom? With your wife or the old father?" asked another.

"Well, since you must know," Nešněra turned to his interlocutor, examining him a few moments as if to decide whether it was worth while to answer him, "with both of them!"

"Ho! ho, poor fellow! That surely is a hot bath when not only one's wife but father as well rip into one," laughed a young man, but the other, an older man, spoke gravely.

"Well, let it be, Frank. It's always better if the wife stands with the old father than against him. And especially at Josifek's house. I don't know what they quarrelled about, but I'll wager the old man wasn't any farther off from the truth than you could make in one jump."

Joseph looked at the speaker disapprovingly, spat through his teeth, shoved his cap further back on his head, and having seated himself, emptied half the glass which the innkeeper placed before him.

"And to prove that I'm a fortune-teller," cried the one who had been called 'Frank,' "I'll tell you the cause of the trouble! It was about the homestead, wasn't it? I'll bet the old man raised the devil, didn't he?"

Old Halama, the neighbor who had previously taken the part of Joseph's father, looked searchingly at the young master of the estate, and when he nodded assent to Frank's "guess," he arose from his chair. Halama's face had become grave and yet simultaneously there appeared a wild cast to his features which an artist might have caught, but which it is impossible to describe.

"What is that, Joseph? Is it really true? Some people said it, but I didn't want to believe it!"

"And why didn't you want to believe it?" young Nešněra braced himself as if for a fight.

"Hold on there! Don't get into that pose with me! You were still a lad looking for mushrooms when I was a comrade of your father's," neighbor Halama admonished Joseph. "But if you want to hear what I didn't want to believe, I'll tell you without stuttering. I couldn't believe that a Nešněra would ever sell the estate on which the blood and sweat as well as the blessings and prayers of generations rest! Do you know, Joseph, what your ancestors suffered, what your father struggled through? And especially your grandfather, God grant him everlasting glory! The German lords were determined to possess your estate, saying it would just suit their needs. They made him offers —promises—but he never gave in. Then they worked up a plot making him out a rebel or something and put him in the dark dungeon of the castle. Each day they took him out to torture him, stretched him on the rack, and after each infliction of terrible physical suffering, they asked him, 'Will you sell by fair means?' But he always replied, 'If you call these "fair means," I'll wait till there are fairer.' And they would have beaten him to death, I believe, if the good Lord Himself hadn't decided to take a hand in things, for once, during the execution of one of their fiendish orders of torture, the Director himself was struck by lightning. The Countess fainted dead away."

"Well and what of it?" cynically asked young Nešněra. "Because my old folks were stubborn headed and didn't understand what was to their own disadvantage, should we be so, too? If someone wants to buy my land and pays well, I can buy elsewhere and it's just as good!"

The neighbors looked breathlessly at old Halama to hear what he would say to that. Some thought that young Nešněra was in the right, others felt, but could not express why they felt, he was wholly wrong.

Old Halama seemed to sense the gravity of the moment. He lost himself in thought for a while, appearing to look off into a corner somewhere and a considerable time elapsed before he spoke.

"You see, Joseph, these are things which are hard to explain by mere reasoning if the heart doesn't listen. The right feeling has to be here under the vest. These are strange things. Perhaps a learned man could find the proper paragraph in books to cover the case, but I don't know any more than the Ten Commandments and what I have written in my heart, 'Honor thy father and thy mother'—and I do honor their work, their sufferings! They did not bequeath me very much, but I value it because it was inherited

FOR THE LAND OF HIS FATHERS 257

from them. Even my very name, Halama,[1] which isn't very pretty, I honor. My great-grandfather received that name from the German overlords because he was indomitable and refused to kiss the lash with which they beat him. And that name given by the nobility to insult him has become my pride. None of my sons is ashamed of his father, even if he is only a Halama—"

"Eh, those are only speeches." Nešněra waved his hand vexedly, drowning his discomfiture in a glass.

"Speeches they are, but not empty ones! No evasions, you understand?" Halama would not permit himself to be interrupted once having gotten into the current. "And it is true that you can do as you please with your own property. You're not sinning against any legal ordinance nor can anyone send you to court for it. But you are committing a sin against your own people on the land of your fathers. What would become of us if everyone renounced his land as easily as you have done? You get rid of it in order to gain a few dollars, another to avoid some misfortune—"

"And soon the Germans would buy up in that way our very mountains beneath our feet," echoed in warm assent Vavřík, one of the young men. "I felt at once that Joseph wasn't doing the right thing. And what's worst of all about it, he's selling the ground for a German school! What do we need of it here?"

---
[1] Halama—a stubborn churl.

"Well, is it to your disadvantage that you know German?" Joseph turned on Vavřík.

"No. It's good to know languages, and the more a person knows the better it is for him. But, for all that, I'm not going to send my children to a German school. No—not for anything! Time enough to learn it when they grow up and go among people as I did. And for that matter, I never studied it. In extreme cases one needs it in trading. But a German school? It isn't that the German teacher instructs in the language—but that he teaches the children to think and feel like Germans. And do you know what that means? You don't, but I'll tell you. It means that some day your boy will be ashamed of his father and of his language and will probably spit upon your grave because he didn't have a better father."

"Ho! ho! ho! It surely won't be quite so bad as that," Jachymek checked him. "You're just saying that because you envy Nešněra since he is to have a neat profit, and not you. What kind of misfortune is— a German school? It doesn't mean that you'll all have to become Germans—and even though it did— what of it? The master wants it because he is a master and a good one. Why didn't some Czech build us a factory here?"

"And so you're going to kiss his hand because he pays you your well-earned wages?"

"That I will, if the time comes!"

"And you don't realize, do you, that that same

hand, through the erection of the factory, struck out of your reach your former greater earnings? You don't seem to figure it out for yourself that from your honest labor you barely eke out a miserable living, while he from your toil makes big capital? And for that paltry wage you want to sell him your blood as well?" queried Vavřík excitedly.

"Say what you please, but a master is a master and he whose bread you eat—well—you know," Jachymek defended himself. "I don't blame Nešněra. He will make money by the deal, will better himself and children, so where's the harm?"

"Well, may it bring him a blessing," old Halama ended the conversation, and started another topic in order to conclude a profitless quarrel during which the heart in his body could hardly keep from quivering to pieces.

III

It was Sunday and work on the fields and in the factory rested. The inhabitants of the village, in part factory hands and in part peasants or really householders who, in addition to their labors on the fields, worked part time in the factory or at home behind the loom, stood around on thresholds with their pipes in their mouths, waiting till the "gentlemen" rode by. It was generally known what would take place at the Nešněras' to-day, and after the custom of people, some condemned, while others commended the young householder for selling his cottage for a school and his lands for the extension of the nobility's park.

Just as had happened yesterday at the inn, so to-day in the village square, various opinions were heard regarding the German school, but of those who found a means of livelihood at the factory, not one ventured to say aloud just what he thought.

Only Makovec, one of those hard mountaineer heads, which when it makes up its mind to push through its ideas, would even have charged a stone wall at full speed, publicly spoke out against it, and when they tried to pacify him, saying someone would inform on him at the German master's, he grew even more furious.

"Yes, indeed! It's a mighty sad thing that we're all bought up, for we're ready to sell one another if the 'master' smiles at us or places us on a better job. There didn't use to be such corruption among us— not even when we were bondmen under the imported German nobility!"

"That's because money is everything now," vigorously assented Halama, who had joined the group. "For money Joseph is selling the roof over his father's head!"

"Well, we haven't yet had a drink on the earnest money. Old Nešněra won't let it come to pass, you'll see!"

While there were plenty of opinions and knowing discussions in the village, at the Nešněras' there was absolute silence. The mistress put the house in order and walked silently from room to room, imploringly trying at times to catch the eye of her husband with her own tearful ones.

She dared not speak. She knew, too, that she could accomplish nothing by words when Joseph had made up his mind about anything. The old man, also, was as if dumb. His face wore a scowl and the son and father passed by each other like dog and cat.

Finally the carriage came rumbling along. The "gentlemen" were coming. The villagers, according to the degree dependent on the factory, greeted them more or less humbly or indifferently, and watched, with pipes in mouths, the passing "nobility." When the carriage stopped and the factory proprietor, Schlosser, with his manager stepped out and entered the gate, the neighbors came from all sides and trooped after them. Halama, Vavřík, Makovec and also Jachymek and a host of others were all there.

The factory owner, Schlosser, expecting a showy greeting, was a little surprised that no one came out to meet him. Joseph was ashamed, though ordinarily he would have gone out on the threshold of his little court to welcome every guest. But to-day he barely opened the door with some timidity and bowed them in.

Schlosser entered with his hat on his head, the manager after him, and then the rest crowded into the doors as tightly as they could.

The factory owner with the affable condescension of

an indulgent ruler to his subjects, made a gesture with his hand towards both old and young Nešněra.

"Well, how is it, old man? Did we come to an agreement?" he asked with a hard foreign accent.

"The gentleman hasn't been making any propositions to me," answered old Nešněra, gazing with significant intimation at Schlosser's hat until the latter grasped the reproach suggested and removed it from his head.

"Good, good!" nodded Nešněra contentedly. "We have on the walls pictures of our sainted protectors and they, at least, deserve that all who enter should bare their heads in greeting!"

A rustle of delight was heard from the doorway.

Schlosser, a little disconcerted, turned vexedly towards the door and asked young Nešněra, "What does this gaping crowd want here?"

"I say, sir," the old man answered for his son, "they are not 'a gaping crowd.' They are neighbors. It's an old custom here that when transactions like this are taking place, we never close the doors before our neighbors. After all, you know, it's the affair of the entire community whether the estate is to be occupied by one of our own kind of people or some alien!"

Schlosser bit his lip, but he did not desire to quarrel with the old man.

"And you? Will you keep your agreement and ride with us?"

"I'll go, gracious sir. I'm only waiting. It's no

use talking to the old man here. After it's all under the seal, he'll give in."

"In order that you two traffickers in human souls may know at once just where you stand," screamed out the old man, "I'll enlighten you! I have things so arranged that if I should not get along with the young people under the same roof, the old drying-kiln over there and the potato field near it will be mine to the day of my death. And from that I will not part even for a thousand, as surely as there is one God above me!"

The factory owner had too good a knowledge of human nature not to realize that all talking was useless here. Old Nešněra stood there, pale, with starting eyes and dishevelled gray hair. He was terrible to look upon. Even Joseph felt very uneasy, and eagerly accepted the master's invitation to depart by reaching for his hat, which was close at hand.

But before the young man could step to the door, his father blocked the way. Old Nešněra in the agony of his heart, perhaps hardly knowing what he was doing, fell on his knees before his son and flung both arms around his knees.

"Joseph, my son!" he cried in a heart-breaking voice. "For the living God, have mercy on my gray head, on yourself and on your own family! Apolenka, children, kneel and implore him! Surely he has not a heart of stone, since a Czech mother gave him birth! Why, it surely cannot be that one Nešněra would heap so much shame on all the rest!"

Both the little boys, not even understanding what it was all about, knelt down beside their grandfather. Apolena, sobbing aloud, leaned against the casement of the door. The neighbors, deeply moved and frowning, pressed forward.

Young Nešněra stood there in painful anxiety and only at Schlosser's beckoning did he recover.

"Let go of me, father, and don't make any scenes! It's all useless!"

"I will not let go," shrieked the old man wildly.

"Let go by fair means!" threateningly shouted the son, incensed that he should be forced into such a humiliating position in the presence of the "master."

"Neither by fair means nor foul!"

But young Nešněra, though he was smaller than his father, with his iron hands tore loose his father's hands clinging to his knees, and pushed him away so roughly that the old man tottered and fell to the floor. Then he quickly followed Schlosser and the manager out to the courtyard and they hastened to enter the carriage.

Old Nešněra picked himself up from the floor and with clenched fists, flying locks of gray, looking more like a specter than a man, ran out after his son. The neighbors who had stepped aside for the gentlemen intercepted his way, fearing that something would happen.

"Let me go, let me go! I'd rather kill him with my own hands than to have him—" ejaculated the old man in a voice resembling the roaring of an animal

FOR THE LAND OF HIS FATHERS 265

more than the tones of a human being. "You're going, Joseph, really going? There is no God above us if you get there safely! And if you sell, my curse goes with you! Do you hear?"

The factory owner urged the coachman to whip up the horses, but, unfortunately, something slipped loose on the harness and it was necessary to first fix it. The screams of Nešněra frightened the horses.

"See—see? God does not wish it!" shrieked the old man, half mad with sorrow.

Vainly the neighbors tried to mollify him. He neither heard nor saw, only fought to pull himself free of their grasp. And when the carriage started to drive away, Nešněra by superhuman strength threw aside those who stood in his way and, seizing a big stone in the yard, threw it after the receding carriage.

A loud scream was heard—Nešněra had struck the manager—but the horses plunged ahead.

"He gave it to him! Lord, but he struck him right! Good for him! Pity he didn't hit the right one!" these and similar exclamations were heard all around.

Nešněra, after this explosion, was like one broken and burst into loud sobbing, refusing to be quieted even after the neighbors had led him into the room.

The evening of the same day a constable came and led away the old man in irons. He made no resistance. Many things had happened that day. Nešněra in grief over his son's treachery had gone to the inn which he had not visited in many years and in his wrath had drunk there beyond temperate measure. He had bitterly reviled his son and had cursed the laws and him who made them.

Rumors of his speeches had reached Schlosser when he returned at noon, bringing Joseph with him as his guest. The factory owner rejoiced with glee that he had so cheaply gotten rid of the obstinate old man. His manager who was quite seriously wounded, remained in the city. And here was a new crime, the crime of insulting His Majesty, the Emperor, which the old man in his wild grief had unthinkingly committed without consideration of consequences.

The factory owner knew he could find enough people who would act as witnesses, and it was he who had sent for the constable.

IV

Hard times came to both of the Nešněras. The old man was locked in jail. The young man had lost all standing both in the village and in his own home. Even those who might have acted as he did now charged him with being the cause of his father's misfortune.

Half the village was secured to testify to this or that crime which the elder Nešněra had committed. Many refused to know anything of what had happened, but when they were threatened with punishment for swearing falsely they talked. There was enough testimony without requiring that of the son. But when he was called he did not dare meet his father's eyes. After they told him he could take advantage of the beneficence of the law not requiring a son to testify against a father, he arose to depart.

That instant his gaze fell on his aged father. The rough mountaineer could not control his emotion. He leaped forward, fell on his knees before his father, and weeping, begged for forgiveness. The people in the courtroom cried, the witnesses, the judge and even the lawyers were touched, but old Nešněra remained like a rock.

"You sold it?" he asked coldly. "Answer—did you sell?"

And when the son dumbly assented, the old man pushed him away so that he staggered towards the bench occupied by the witnesses.

"Go then, go! Accursed! I no longer have a son, nor you a father! But when they let me go from here—"

He was not permitted to speak further. They led his son away from the courtroom. This cruel scene impressed the judge and jury unfavorably, but in the course of the trial, they again were inclined towards the stubborn old man who had wished to preserve his inherited estate for his descendants. Their decree was fairly light. He was sentenced to ten months in prison. When the attorney explained to Nešněra that it was absolutely the minimum sentence for two such serious crimes, the convicted man announced that he accepted the penalty and was ready to suffer it.

Those ten months sped as if in winged flight. Old Nešněra, returning one day to his native village, was nearly petrified to find a new building in the place where his little home used to stand.

The old man, bent by grief and suffering, straightened up fiercely at the unexpected sight.

"Oh, is that you, Nešněra? Welcome home," sounded a hearty voice. "We didn't expect you till day after to-morrow."

Nešněra silently extended his hand to Halama and with the other pointed to the building.

"It makes your eyes bulge, doesn't it? That's the new school—a German one! You'll see the inscription. Schlosser made haste—speeded up the building of it! In a few days it's to be consecrated. And say, old comrade! There'll be children in plenty there—over half of the village. The factory hands and many of the others in some way employed by our German 'gentlemen' got a sort of insight that it was vain to resist!"

"And that's what my son did for you people! You must all curse him for it!"

"Well, I haven't yet heard anyone praise him."

"And what about my reserved portion and cottage? Have they torn that down, too?" Nešněra asked in menacing tones.

"No, they didn't do that. Your son had it fixed up.

FOR THE LAND OF HIS FATHERS

Wants to get reconciled with you. And your daughter-in-law saw to it that everything was made as attractive as possible for you. They themselves live here in the school. Joseph has a sign over his door, 'School Janitor,' but it's in German, in big letters, 'Schuldiener.' You'll be surprised!"

"Well, I'll not see it," said the old man, but immediately fell into thought. A queer idea flashed into his head.

"So you say the school's to be consecrated in a week? Well, I won't carry the holy water for them during the ceremony." Without any words of parting, he left Halama, entered the yard and directed his course straight to the old drying kiln which now was newly whitewashed and tastefully prepared inside.

"Joseph, Schuldiener," cried Halama in muffled tones, tapping at the window. "Your old father has returned and has gone to his 'cottage.'"

There was a movement inside the room and Apolenka came running out to greet her father-in-law and take him to his new abode. Joseph did not yet have the courage.

V

A peculiar change came over old Nešněra. He never had been very loquacious, but from the time he returned from prison he never spoke a word with anyone. He would pat his daughter-in-law and grandchildren on the head, but he never offered his hand to his son, and when the latter tried to make friends with him he always turned away.

"A silent madman!" they repeated throughout the village. "Poor fellow! His grief went to his head. And no wonder!"

"But what will it be when he sees the celebration of the school consecration?"

"He won't see it! He'll lock himself in his room and won't crawl out."

The great day of the school consecration arrived. The factory proprietor, Schlosser, exerted every effort to arrange a big celebration. He distributed an immense number of flags throughout the community, mainly the black-and-yellow emblem, but also a few red-and-white ones. He himself went from house to house. He promised the parish priest to secure funds for alterations on the church. He gave his word to the mayor that he would personally be responsible for the repair of the public highways, which improvement the citizens had been unable to secure from the county directors. To others he gave promises of this or that sort, to the doubters he gave ready money, but to his factory employees he merely gave orders to be on hand.

Schlosser had determined that he must triumph in vauntingly ostentatious fashion over the obstinate old Czech. And he did triumph.

On the day of the celebration the entire village, with the exception of a few out-and-out old-fashioned Czechs, was all rejoicing and excitement from early dawn. Be-

FOR THE LAND OF HIS FATHERS 271

yond the church where the procession was forming, they were firing from mortars and bands played merrily.

Everyone came—the factory foremen and their wives, the district officials from the city, the priest, the schoolmaster and nearly all the villagers. The village itself was wholly deserted and at Nešněra's, that is at the school building, there was not a living soul.

At that hour, old Nešněra emerged from his cottage and directed his steps to the schoolhouse. He wished to enter through the main door, but found it locked. In the celebration program, Schlosser was to hand over the key which had been gilded for the occasion, to the mayor of the community.

A window in the lower part of the structure had been left open and through that the old man with the nimbleness of a youth slipped inside. Then he quickly closed the window and went forward into the main hall. Moved by a strange thought, he approached the door and slid the bolt so that not even by the aid of a key could anyone enter the building. Then he inspected the hall. The inscription on the wall met his gaze. It was in German, but Nešněra could understand it. It read "Everything depends on God's blessing."

"Just wait, I'll give you a blessing," he muttered, shaking his fist. He turned and saw a crucifix on the wall. He fell on his knees before it and prayed for a long time. Then he arose, his eyes shining with an odd light, and betook himself to the upper floor, thence to the garret.

If someone had passed the school at that moment, they would have seen the black-and-yellow banner which had been waving from the dormer window disappear. Almost immediately, however, the heavy flag staff was restored.

Beyond the village the firing of mortars was heard, the music began and the procession, now fully formed, started on its jubilant march towards the school. At that instant, old Nešněra, with eyes fairly starting from their sockets, was kneeling in prayer near the dormer window.

He knelt with clasped hands, his lips repeating the prayer of the dying. And when he realized that the procession had already turned into the main street leading to the school and that in the next moment they would be here, he rose and suddenly leaped out.

The factory proprietor, Schlosser, cursed loudly and turned to "Schuldiener" Nešněra, demanding to know what had become of the black-and-yellow flag. The eyes of all turned towards the dormer, but without warning something most remarkable appeared there. An unrecognizable figure dropped out of the dormer window and then, intercepted in its fall by a rope, swung back and forth like a pendulum from the flag staff. Later they distinguished that it had hands which were wildly gesticulating.

"Christ Jesus! It is he! It is the old man!" echoed from every pair of lips, and the participants in the celebration parade in excited haste flew to the school. The music became silent, but the mortars kept on booming in exultant triumph.

"The key! Quick, give me the key!" screamed Joseph like one stark mad, rushing at Schlosser. Apolenka burst into sobs, the children set up a wail, Schlosser uttered oath after oath, while his wife, beholding the horrible scene, sank to the ground and rolled about in spasms.

In vain did Joseph try to enter the school. The throng of people meantime gazed at the corpse of the old man which still swung in the breeze. His face, around which fluttered his long gray locks and white beard, took on in the death struggle a terrible appearance. The cheeks became ashy, the eyes were rolled up and from the open mouth the tongue protruded.

Women shrieked and covered their eyes with their hands. Men called for the firemen with their ladders until it occurred to someone to break open a window and jump inside.

An instant later the flag-post with the corpse of Nešněra was drawn back into the dormer. They untied his body and began at once to try to resuscitate him, but it was useless.

Nešněra was with his God!

VI

A year had passed since the death of Nešněra, but in the school no teaching had begun, although the teacher was there and all the equipment needed for instruction. The horrible death of Nešněra had so reacted on the minds of all that not a single inhabitant of the village arrived to register in the new school.

Schlosser tried to compel his employees, but they all threatened that they would rather hang themselves. And from that time he had a horror of hanged persons. Often in his dreams he saw the apparition of the old man whom he had driven to death. Schlosser's wife paid for that deed in the loss of her health. She nearly lost her life also, but as it was, the life of her child which came into the world prematurely was the price paid.

And it was this woman, broken until the end of her days, who had been accustomed to look upon the laboring class contemptuously and without sympathy, who now implored her husband with clasped hands not to force his workmen into the German school.

Finally, even Schlosser himself began to believe, although he would never acknowledge it, that fate had avenged itself on him.

But things went harder with Joseph, whom no one addressed otherwise than as "Schuldiener." He seemed to have lost wife, children and love of life. He gave himself up to drinking and whenever he was much intoxicated he cursed and reviled himself, the German "master," the church and even the school. Often he threatened that he would settle his score with Schlosser.

But Schlosser one day just before he departed with

his wife for some place in Italy, called the mayor of the village and announced to him that he wished to present the school building to the community on condition that the adjoining lands and the former habitation of Nešněra, together with the sheds and outbuildings, should remain the possession of the grandchildren of the hanged suicide.

When young Nešněra heard of it, he burst into bitter sobbing, and throwing himself down upon the earth kissed and caressed it. They could not even tear him from it.

"My beloved land! Blood and sweat of my fathers! Preserved for us! And the Nešněras shall not die out here! But a certain one of them this land must no longer bear on its bosom!"

When he arose from the ground, a strange light gleamed in his deepset, bloodshot eyes.

The next day they found Nešněra dead on the grave of his father. He had shot himself in order that he should no more desecrate by a single step that soil of which he had proved himself unworthy.

VII

The school on the Nešněra homestead stands to this day. And it prospers for it is teaching children to love their native country, their nation and the land of their fathers. The factory, too, is still there and in operation, but Schlosser's son never influences his employees by a single word to deny their nationality.

Beyond the school, Nešněra's wife, with the money left her after the death of her husband, built a new cottage for her children. The older one of the boys when he had grown up and attended the required schools, became teacher in "Nešněra's school." The younger one devoted himself to farming the home fields and thus both remained on the native soil of their fathers.

To-day the older of the two is in charge of the schools, for the community has grown and prospered and there was need of more teachers for the increased number of children. The younger brother became mayor of the town. Both are the most zealous advocates of love for that land which our fathers by the sweat of their brows have earned and by their blood have hallowed for us as our heritage. And, in truth, I think that in that community it would be impossible for an enemy outsider to buy enough land to hold so much as a post on which the one selling it might follow the example of old Nešněra.

CAROLINE SVĚTLÁ

(Born 1830 in Prague.   Died 1899, Prague.)

This gifted authoress, whose maiden name was Johanna Rottova, called by Dr. J. Bačkovský the greatest of the more recent novelists devoting themselves almost exclusively to typical Bohemian backgrounds, was the child of a Czech father and a Czech-German mother. She had early to go through a painful nationalistic struggle, being born in sadly backward surroundings, but her marriage at the age of twenty-two to Prof. Peter Mužák strengthened her deep patriotic self-consciousness. In the home of her husband in the mountains of Ještěd, she first met with the striking and rugged mountaineer types so well described in her collections of stories entitled "Sketches from Ještěd." She chose her pen name from the name of the mountain village which she so often visited—"Světlá" below Ještěd.

Her first novel "Two Awakenings" was published in 1858. Since then she has been almost feverishly active in her literary effort, bringing out her intense convictions on female education and advancement, national consciousness, and other subjects in a series of many novels and short stories. Chief among her works are "První Češka" (The First Czech Woman), and "Na Úsvitě" (At Dawn) both of which depict the period of the Czech renaissance; "Několik Archů z Rodinné Kroniky" (Some Pages from Family Chronicles), "Lamač a Jeho Dítě" (The Quarryman and His Child), "Vesnický Román" (A Village Romance) and "Kříž u Potoka" (The Cross Beside the Brook), —these latter two dramatized by Eliška Pešková and "Hubička" (The Kiss) dramatized by E. Krásnohorská. "Poslední Paní Hlohovská" (The Last Lady of Hlohov) a novel of the Thirty Years War and of the court of Joseph II, has been translated into English under the title of "Maria Felicia."

Světlá is always sincere and direct and seldom varies in her style. She has a story to tell that is worth reading and in no case does she tax the limits of plausibility to induce interest. Her stories are of her own people, in whose happiness she rejoiced, in whose sufferings she sorrowed.

BARBARA

BY CAROLINE SVĚTLÁ

It caused much mirth among the people that Matýsek and Barka[1] wished to get married! She almost reached to the ceiling, whereas when he sat down to the table, his head was barely visible above it. She laughed from morn till eve, whereas he was always pouting. She would have charged ten Prussians single-handed, while he dropped his eyes and blushed a deep red whenever anyone glanced at him without warning. Barka was always contented with things as they were—in whatever form they came, she accepted them. When things were at the worst, she would remark, "Well, never mind!" and soon forgot her trouble. Matýsek, on the contrary, remembered things for a long time and at even a trivial circumstance he would whine, "Too much is too much!"

Whenever people saw them together, they always marvelled how these two came to care for each other.

It began when they were both still watching flocks. They used to drive their herds to the same pasture. As soon as Matýsek's two goats were feeding, he paid

[1] In the title of the story here given Světlá has used the name "Barbara" from which "Barka" as used in the story is a derivative or abbreviation.

attention to nothing else, but sat down somewhere under a bush, found a stick, drew out his pocket knife and began to whittle out something.

But the other boys would not permit this. They wanted everyone who used the same pasture with them to play the same sort of pranks they did. If Matýsek did not wish to obey them—and he often didn't—they would snatch his knife, throw it away and break whatever he had just carved out. The more he pouted and growled about it, the more they made wry faces at him, as is customary in such mischievous groups.

But as soon as Barka from a distance noted that the boys were teasing Matýsek, she ran directly to a tree, broke off a goodly branch, and rushed after the boys. She barely glanced around when she was among them and where the bough struck was all one to her—why had they not left Matýsek in peace?

"This is for remembrance! And if it seems too little to some of you, just come, I'll give you plenty more till you've had enough," she would shout after them when, with much squalling, they dispersed in all directions. Then she seated the whimpering Matýsek back under his bush, found his knife for him and sought out the pieces of wood. After such a distribution of punishment, Matýsek had a fine time at the pasture for a week at least.

To be sure, the boys did not let it pass without comment that Barka always protected Matýsek.

"There, there," they shouted at her when she was

quieting his wailing. "Put him away nicely into a box so that the birds may not swallow him in place of a fly. If a grasshopper tramples him to death, it will be all up with your wedding and we'd lose out on our gifts."

But the instant they saw Barka raising the switch they were off with the wind and ran until their heads shook. They had ample proof that Barka had the strength of fifteen of them and they knew they could not overcome her even if all of them at once pitched into her.

Matýsek was in the service of a childless old widow who was no longer able to get about on her feet and whose sight was very dim. She was satisfied with the amount of work he did and the way he did it, and never cheated him out of food. She was glad she had a helper who did not cheat her. Nevertheless, Matýsek often complained that no one had it as hard as did he, and that too much was too much.

Barka served on the estate of the worst pinch-penny in the entire neighborhood. Her fingers were like jagged pegs from sheer hard work, all the veins in her neck were swollen and her face was so burned from the sun and wind that her skin was always peeling. She served him each year in return for ten yards of linen cloth for a waist and a loose jacket and for one pair of winter shoes. Instead of wages he let her have small tips whenever he sold a head of cattle from his stables or when she carried the corn to the mill, and yet she found cause for praises.

"Not a day passes but what the peasant gives me food," she said delightedly to Matýsek. "And I have shoes to wear to church. Since I've been on his estate I have provided myself with two heavy wool head shawls, one skirt and one coat. I don't have to wear my linen jacket on Sundays if I don't wish to."

And Barka was in the tenth year of her service at the miserly peasant's.

Sometimes people laughed about the attachment of the two and then again they asserted, also laughingly, to be sure, that the two just suited each other as if the pigeons had borne them. By which they meant that one was about as weak mentally as the other.

If anyone let drop a whisper of such an insinuation before Barka, she let it stand as far as it applied to herself, replying only with her customary, "Never mind!" But God forbid that anyone should so express himself about Matýsek. She was up in arms immediately.

"You just let Matýsek alone," she shouted till she was fairly purple. "He has sense enough for himself and he doesn't have to have it for others."

Matýsek never so violently opposed anyone who had anything against Barka or himself, but it never was erased from his memory. If he had to pass near such a person, he dropped his eyes and would not have raised them if he had known that he'd be shot for it. Yes, Matýsek had his own head and knew how to set it and also how to punish people whom he had cause to dislike.

At the dances none of the girls wished to be Matýsek's partner, claiming he wasn't grown up enough and was unhandsome and scowly. Besides, he had nothing to dress up in except the jacket left him by his deceased father, and they said his vest showed for a good hand's length beneath the jacket, which was decorated with buttons as big as one's fist. They had other faults to find with him also, but this did not worry him, for he always managed to dance to his heart's content without them. Barka always sought out Matýsek at the dances herself. She held him by the hands as a mother does her one-year-old when she is teaching him to stand up like a little man, and thus she danced with him as long as his breath lasted. She herself never ran out of breath, even if she had remained on the dancing floor all night.

But it was no real pleasure or gratification to dance with Matýsek, for he did not know one note from another and never seemed to get into step. He hopped about as best he could, hanging his head and inclining his whole body forward. If his partner had not held him firmly, who knows how many times he would have had to kiss the floor in an evening. But Barka made up for it by bobbing up all the higher and the more merrily beside him, looking about over the whole room meanwhile to see if everyone was taking proper notice of how well Matýsek could guide. During the entire dance she smiled happily, showing her white teeth. The people fairly held their sides when watching these two dance.

"Why do you persist in dancing with such a clumsy fellow? You trip so lightly and we'd like to take you for a few turns ourselves," the boys shouted to Barka, but only in mockery and never in earnest, just to see what she would say. They would not have taken her to dance for a great deal unless they intended to insult and anger their own sweethearts.

But Barka always cut them off sharply.

"Just you take whomever you please for a turn. I'll keep Matýsek and I'll not let you abuse him either. He knows how to weave an Easter whip of forty strands, he can make a broom, and a battledore for a shuttlecock as well. Everybody doesn't have to go ramming his head into idlers for beauty or to crush rocks with their hands."

And again she was with Matýsek in the whirl and whoever failed to turn briskly enough, him would she take by the elbow and shove out so effectually that he wondered what world he was in and how he got there. Matýsek was much pleased with Barka's agility and he continued in low whispers to indicate others for her to jostle out of the circle, chuckling meanwhile till he nearly choked. He used to say to Barka afterwards when he escorted her home that he wouldn't want another girl, not even for all of Jerusalem, and that he'd stay faithful to her even if brides from Prague itself would send him word to come to marry them.

If Matýsek's mistress gave him cheese on his bread at the Sunday meal, he ate the bread and saved the cheese for Barka. If on Sunday Barka received a muffin at the peasant's, she at once put it aside for Matýsek. As soon as Matýsek had washed his wooden spoon after dinner, he threw off his linen blouse and put on the red vest he had inherited from his father, and over it he drew the blue jacket which was so displeasing to the girls.

Barely had Barka finished milking after dinner when she slipped on her starched skirt, placed one of her wool kerchiefs on her head, another around her neck and went to meet Matýsek.

She knew to a hair when he would come, although they never made a definite arrangement. He, in turn, not only knew well that she would come, but just in what spot among the trees he would first see her.

"You wouldn't go to meet any other man, would you?" he used to ask after they met.

"Not for seven golden castles," Barka assured him.

It was really remarkable how devoted they were. Never had a youth or maid cared for each other as did those two who seemed to have but one soul in common.

When it was cold or rainy, they sat down beside each other in the stable. When it was bright and sunny, they seated themselves somewhere on the boundary stones. He reached into his pocket and drew out the cheese neatly wrapped in a large walnut leaf, while she unfolded her fresh white handkerchief and gave him the muffin. They ate and sunned themselves, but if it happened to be warm, they took a little nap or at other times they got into such an earnest conversation that they did not know how to end it. Matýsek knew how to lead one into strange discussions and often Barka shivered in wonderment at him.

For instance, if, from their position on the boundary line, he saw a carriage approaching on the highway, he would begin conjecturing who rode in it, whether the steward from the court, the brewer from the city or, perhaps, the Prince himself.

"There ought to be a law against certain people always riding while others must continually go on foot and also against some persons having great wealth while others have nothing," Matýsek reasoned between conjectures.

"The court will hardly make a law against such things," was Barka's opinion.

"I'm quite sure the rich men won't permit such a law," grinned Matýsek. And to think that people said he was weak mentally!

"Perhaps if God wished it, it would come to pass," judged Barka. "But most likely it isn't the law because it wouldn't agree with everyone's health."

Matýsek remained firm, however, that a law should be enacted making it possible for all people to ride in carriages and from that stand he refused to budge. But Barka nevertheless tripped him up on the matter.

"And who, good friend, would then look after the horses? Who would water and feed them?"

Matýsek could not quickly answer and remained

for a long time looking at Barka with wide eyes and open mouth. He evaded giving a direct reply by expressing the wish that he might some day have so much money that at every step it would jingle in his pocket.

"It will all come to you," Barka encouraged him.

"Oh, no, it won't," complained Matýsek, but at the same time he wanted Barka to assure him again.

"Yes, indeed, it will come," she reiterated. "Isn't it already beginning for you? It is commencing for me, too. We have quite a bit of money out among people, and if we are alive and well, we can get the good of it."

"Where did you say we had money?"

"Why, at our masters'. If we have health and serve them for twenty years yet, no mere hundred will cover what they owe us. Just count it up!"

"Wait," pouted Matýsek. "You're making sport of me." But he couldn't frown very long and had to smile a little at least at the way in which Barka had turned the matter. It seemed as if she were poking fun at him and yet what she said was true. And, indeed, taken all around, Barka was right. Seeing that he was prepared to smile, Barka began to laugh also and Matýsek joined in heartily, while they figured how much money they had out among people and how rich they were.

But in the midst of her laughter, Barka's eyes filled with tears.

"One thing, at least, was fulfilled for my dear mother," she sobbed, trying to smile at the same time. "She always used to tell me, 'I can bequeath nothing to you, but may God grant that you may inherit one trait from me. I don't know how to be angry and I can always find the bright side of everything I meet—let it be what it will.'"

Matýsek's eyes were wet also. When he could not see her laugh without smiling himself, it is not to be wondered at that he could not see her cry without weeping with her! I have already said that in those two beings there was but one soul.

"There's nothing on this earth I wish for," sobbed Barka, "but one thing and that is, that I might some day go to Vambeřice. It is there my mother offered me to the Holy Virgin and there she prayed that I might inherit her good nature."

"Some day you'll get your wish," Matýsek now in turn comforted Barka. "And perhaps much more, besides," he added, and he was glad he thought of it as a means of bringing her out of her tears.

"Do you think I'll some day be able to have a green jacket with a sulphur-yellow border?" sighed Barka, wiping her eyes with her work-calloused hands. "I must say I'd dearly love to have something pretty in which to go to Communion."

"And wouldn't you like to have a goat of your own, and a little cottage, too?" Matýsek inquired of her searchingly.

"Why wouldn't I want a goat and a home of my own? Of course, I'd want it. But, believe me, if I could really have a house, I'd not give in an inch unless I'd have hanging beside the stove a spoon rack, painted a blood red and made for eight sizes, with four pewter spoons in each."

"And if I had my own room," Matýsek cried, seeming to have grown a head taller, "I, too, would know what I want. At once I'd quit all peasant toil and would begin weaving brooms. That's something worth while. A man can sit in the warmth and where it's clean and can keep busy at his own work. Everyone inquires after him and knows of him. Nobody can get along without a broom-maker."

"That's true," Barka nodded assent. "To be a broom-maker is a very fine thing. I, too, like that trade."

"I wouldn't spend all my time making brooms," boasted Matýsek and again he seemed to have grown much taller. "I'd also make wooden lanterns and would fit in the glass sides myself, and if anyone wanted a cage for quails, I'd make it for him and attach a little bell at the top. I'd go in for making a dog-kennel as well. I'd paint it green and to make it please everybody, I'd fix on it a blue star and a little yellow moon. Don't you think I couldn't do it. I could!"

If some one from the village passed by and saw them sitting beside each other debating so fervently, he did not fail to pause and ask them, "When, good people, do you intend to get married?"

"Oh, some day," Barka dispatched the inquisitive one.

"It's high time. You were courting when I was wooing my wife and now I have a son almost ready for marrying—"

"Well, everything doesn't have to be done in a rush. What awaits a man will come to him of itself."

"That's all true, but a man must set some limit of time for doing everything."

"Well, then, it will be when our masters mention it to us."

"You'll have a long wait!"

"Never mind! We're not in any hurry just now."

Matýsek never answered such questions, but always remembered everyone who approached them in this matter. A hundred times such an inquirer might pass or call to him, but each time he would drop his eyes and not lift them until the mocker was past.

How did Barka guess that whatever awaits a man will come to him of itself? Everything that they had ever wished for and which they had discussed on Sunday afternoons was fulfilled for them with the exception of one little point. Would anyone have said that such things are possible? Never!

Barka's cousin who had never claimed relationship to her died. She had been a strange woman. She had but one daughter with whom she lived in great ill-will because the young woman had married someone whom the mother disliked. She let her daughter move away with her husband far beyond the borders, but never made inquiries about her and when a letter came from her she refused it. The mother and daughter had not known of each other for many years.

When, after the death of the mother, the court wrote to the daughter to come and claim her inheritance, it developed that she was long since dead and her husband also. No children remained and as there were no other relatives, everything fell to Barka. Of a sudden, she owned a house, an orchard, a little field and meadow, two goats in the stall, all sorts of cabinet and carpenter material, and in the chamber two chests full of clothing. In one were suits which had belonged to her deceased cousin's husband. He had been a carpenter and dressed very well. Among these possessions remained a fur coat and a blue top coat as handsome as if the tailor had brought it that very day. As soon as Barka opened the second chest the first thing she saw was a green jacket with a border as yellow as sulphur.

Beneath the jacket lay so many skirts that Barka could have put on a different one every day in the week, though she would not have done this for the whole world. She had too great a fear of God.

When Barka first heard of her inheritance she was so stunned that they had to pinch her arms to make her come to her senses, and it was no wonder, for it really was unbelievable. She continued to stand motionless, unable to comprehend that what had been her cousin's was now to be hers and that never again did she need to be a servant—nor Matýsek either.

"Do get some wisdom in you," the master of the place urged. "If you'll be as stupid as this, people will soon deprive you of what the Lord has lavished on you. I already see in my mind's eye how you will let yourself get cheated until you will again have nothing. I must myself intervene so that you'd not complain some day that I had no more sense than you. It will be best if you get married and that very soon. I can readily tell you of a bridegroom who will very carefully attend to all the matters concerning your property and you yourself will not have to pay any attention to them." And the peasant named his own brother who about a year before had lost his wife. People said that he beat his wife to death. He was known as a bully far and wide. If a person just barely looked at him, having no evil intention whatever, he called him in the ring for a fight. People went a hundred feet out of the way to avoid him. His children all took after him and were as evil as their father. The peasant was afraid that his brother might some day kill someone and, should he be sentenced to prison, the degenerate children would come into his home. He would much rather wish them upon Barka.

They had to resuscitate Barka again, for his speech frightened her so.

"How can you talk to me of your brother, when you know that I have Matýsek!" she rebuked him, trembling all over.

"Surely you don't intend, now that you have property, to tie yourself to that hungry, half-dead mortal who has nothing and never will have, to the day of his death? He was good enough while no one else wanted you."

You should have seen how Barka flared up! She flushed with anger and every nerve in her body was strained.

"The man I wasn't good enough for before this," burst violently from her lips, "isn't good enough for me now. Matýsek has wanted me for years and never cared for another. Even if a bride from Prague had sent for him, he wouldn't have married her for all of Jerusalem, and you think I'd consider another man now? No, not for seven golden castles, not even if my own patron saint made the match. Indeed, not even for the sake of the Virgin Mary would I forsake him.—That is my vow!"

And Barka became almost ill at the idea of being torn away from Matýsek. When she got breath enough, she set up such a wailing about Matýsek that it could be heard to the village square. She was not to be quieted, and the peasant, though he kept on trying to persuade her in order to provide for his hectoring brother and wicked children, could do nothing with her. He left her in great wrath, seeing at last that she would not yield, but he did not speak a single word to her any more while she was there.

Matýsek, however, was not in the least astonished at the turn affairs had taken. Why, had not Barka long promised these things? They had been awaiting it, talking of it, finally it was actually here, so what was there strange or unusual about it? Indeed, he wondered why it hadn't come to them long ago. It never once occurred to him that perhaps now he might not be desirable to Barka. People here and there hinted it to him in envy, but he laughed in their faces. He— not to be desirable to Barka! For her there was no one else on earth so well suited.

Barka stood staring at him when he announced that he was going to the parsonage to order their banns. She could not comprehend where he had suddenly accumulated so much boldness. As soon as she told him to go if he thought best, he adjusted himself deliberately and then strode through the village to the priest so energetically that the latter thought it was some fine gentleman coming to him. From the time he heard his banns proclaimed in the church, Matýsek never got out of people's way, but, on the contrary, others stepped aside for him. God alone can judge where by a hand's turn he acquired the ability to act the part of a great man. Those who had not seen him for a long time and now met him did not know in what manner to address him. In a word, he was totally changed from his former self.

Barka inherited with the property a female tenant with four children. She was happy over this and at once embraced the little ones in her love, remembering her own widowed mother and the days of her orphaned childhood. But Matýsek was different.

He examined the widow and her children with an eye so severe that the tenant involuntarily hid behind Barka and the children began to shake with fear. Then he inquired if they understood properly who and what he was. When the poor things did not know what to answer, he told them that he was master in the home and that everyone must obey him, and when he ordered something done in the house or on the field or in the stable, it must be carried out to the hair. In order to confirm this by example, he sent out each child successively about five times for something or other which he had no use for and which the child then had to carry back.

The children hardly dared to breathe.

"You'd like it, wouldn't you?" continued Matýsek. "All day to be in idleness, to fear no one or nothing? But I'll spoil all that for you. I'll give you exercises and training until I teach you order."

Barka was not at all opposed, for why shouldn't he speak up to the children if it pleased him? And besides, even if he shouted, it didn't injure them, and then, how grandly it suited him to act lordly!

The first day after the wedding she gave him an ample supply of coins to jingle in his pocket. He would not permit the children to even come near that day, and on Sunday, when he put on his top coat, they did not dare even look at it for fear they'd soil it.

Matýsek now whirled about proudly in a clean, warm room into which he'd call the children ten times a day to hear them repeat who was master in the house and from which he would ten times expel them for the most varied crimes such as disrespectful coughing or sneezing in his presence, but mainly for silence when he questioned them regarding his own importance and significance. Some days the children did little else than open the door to each other in a succession of such "exercises."

Barka did not cease to marvel at the fortune which was theirs, especially when her eyes fell on the wall beside the stove, where hung a spoon rack, painted red, made for eight sizes and four pewter spoons on each, the kind she had always longed for. Sometimes she gazed at them for an hour at a time. She and Matýsek now ate only with pewter spoons and from porcelain dishes. They did not have a single wooden spoon nor wooden bowl in the whole house. Neither was there anything else of mean and lowly associations to be found in their dwelling from attic to cellar. It was not to be wondered at that Matýsek would not permit it and that Barka gave her consent.

Matýsek carried out his oft-repeated intentions, and renouncing all peasant labor, began weaving brooms. He would not let Barka go to pasture the cattle nor for wood to the grove. The tenant had to see to all this and Barka dared do nothing else but prepare meals and sit beside him and spin. He wanted her to have him before her constantly and to admire him.

Barka often wondered not only that he wished this but that he was so truly in earnest about it. He made not only brooms, but lanterns, cages and anything his fancy suggested. Many people now knew of Matýsek and sought him out. It was just as he had predicted— he had become a notable. Often he related to the children that all this was just what he had anticipated when Barka used to take his part while they were both pasturing flocks. At the same time, he admonished them to be mindful of his every word and deed so that they too might some day follow in his footsteps, but he had great fears that such a result would not really be attained, for, not in a single trait did the children resemble him.

When the children had to hop about Matýsek practically all day, and, as the whim struck him, had to rush away or come speeding back, to speak or remain silent, to place things within his reach or to remain motionless at a safe distance, Barka would often secretly supply them with dainties which their mother could not have provided. She did this in order that they should the more willingly do his bidding. But Matýsek was not supposed to know of any such proceeding and Barka had to exercise the greatest caution. Whenever Matýsek learned of such a gift, he pouted and whimpered: "Couldn't you have given it to me? It would have done me more good than them."

The doghouse with the star and the moon ornaments which Matýsek had joyously planned on for so long, he made for himself.

"Why shouldn't we ourselves have something unusual?" he said to Barka. And he bought a dog to put in the kennel. Although it was a white dog, he called it "Gypsy." His former mistress had a dog named "Gypsy" and he could not break himself of the habit of calling every dog by that name.

When the weather was windy or stormy, Matýsek would lose himself in thought for two hours at a time.

"What have you in your head again?" Barka would ask, smiling proudly meanwhile. She knew he was planning something that no one else would have thought of. And she was right.

"I was debating whether a person could make some sort of cage or trap to catch the wind and hold it. That would be an advantage to us in our mountains here, wouldn't it, our Barka?"

From the time they had married, they never addressed each other otherwise than "our Barka" and "our Matýsek."

Barka assented that it would indeed be a great convenience for people to entrap the wind so that it would do no harm.

"Well, who knows? You may work it out successfully," she often said. "When people have been able to catch and chain the lightning and thunder and it submits, why shouldn't you be able to devise a cage to catch the wind?"

Sometimes Matýsek would suddenly cast aside the broom he was making and would stretch himself out on the bench behind the table.

"I don't have to work if I don't want to, do I, our Barka? No one has a right to give orders to me nor to you either. Leave your spinning and come, sit beside me at the table. Let's have a game of cards, a little smoke and a bit of something to drink."

"Well, why not?" Barka agreed with him, and leaving her spinning wheel, she went to the cupboard for pipes, cards and glasses. The pipes were lighted, Barka poured some bitter brandy into the glasses, shuffled the cards and they played, smoked and sipped to their hearts' content. As a matter of fact, Matýsek at first did not even know how to play cards or smoke, and it was all he could do to swallow the bitter brandy, for he was accustomed only to whey. But Barka kept telling him that he would always miss something if he did not learn to take a drink now and then, to play cards and smoke. Finally he consented to try it. But she had to agree to try it all with him, for without her he would none of it, and when she wished to have him continue at it as was fitting for a fully qualified master of an estate who expects the esteem of people, he would not have it otherwise than that she, too, should continue beside him smoking and sipping.

Hardly had Barka fully arranged her new household, when she thought of Vamberice. She was of the opinion that her planet poured fortune on her only because her mother had offered her in sacrifice at Vamberice.

Matýsek could hardly wait till she returned from the pilgrimage. Even the first day he ran to the window every little while to see if she were already coming back. In order to have the time go more rapidly, he kept pushing the clock ahead and made marks on the door to indicate how many days she had been gone and how soon she was certain to return.

"Too much is too much," he grumbled, impatiently, returning alone to his room. During all that time, he never touched the cards, pipe or glasses, and even refused to look at his brooms. The tenant could not suit him by a single glance or act. Barka had arranged for her to cook for Matýsek in her absence, but he found fault with everything that she prepared and brought to the table.

The children, however, fared the worst of all. They barely crossed his path when he started after them with a switch and drove them out. If they were not around him, he went looking for them with a rod, inquiring why they were not at hand to do his bidding. So it went constantly just as in a comedy. The sun was still high, when he would cry out to the tenant, "Have those children say their prayers and put them to bed so there would be some peace!" She had hardly heard them repeat their prayers and put them on their beds of hay when he burst out on her with a tirade for bringing up her children as lazy lollers who will never know anything but how to sleep and surely would come to some evil end. He roused such fears in the woman with his predictions of a terrible death for her children that she herself seized the whip and drove the children from the hay. Half asleep they were forced to seat themselves beside her around the old tilted-up cask, used to hold cabbage, and she compelled them to strip chicken feathers for down for the winter. They stripped for hours till both children and mother, together with the tub, toppled over on the floor, where they slept exhausted from very fear, continual running and uneasiness until the next morning, when the treadmill began anew.

Barka had her hands full to again bring about order when she returned. They had all lost flesh, in fact, were fairly ill and from all sides came only complaints and accusations in which she had the hard task of acting as judge. She made an end to all at once by vowing with uplifted hand that she would never again go away on a pilgrimage. At that time the poor thing did not know that she had near at hand another pilgrimage from which there is no returning.

Without any previous warning, Barka's hand began to swell.

"It must be because I am no longer doing any real work," she said to Matýsek. "All the strength stays in my hand and that's why it is swelling. It isn't healthy for anyone to be lazy. I said that to you more than once when we were both single and you used to wish that all the people could just ride around in carriages and do nothing."

The tenant did not like the looks of the hand. It seemed to her that it was somehow caused from the bone.

"Just as soon as the snow melts, I'm going beyond the mountains to get you a doctor. He is very much renowned and doesn't ask too much money either."

"Let him ask what he will, I'll count it out for him here on the table," boasted Matýsek, jingling the coins in his pocket. He was grieved that Barka seemed to grow weaker from the afflicted hand and had to lie down every little while. When he did not have her beside him, he was lonely. They had to move her bed right under the very window so that she could see him clearly and he could look at her.

The tenant did not wait for the snow to melt, but at the first gleam of a warmer sun, when a little break could be seen through the windows in the orchard, she started out, over the mountains, not minding the snowdrifts and safely reached the doctor whom she brought back with her to Barka.

The doctor examined the swollen hand, drew out from his case some sort of oil and ordered that she should diligently rub it on the hand. If the oil did not help, she was to notify him and he would send some kind of liquid which would surely bring relief. But he did not fool Barka.

She read in his eyes after he had examined her hand and looked significantly at the tenant that no oil or salve would help her. She knew that she would never again rise to her feet a healthy woman. The tenant was right—the bone in her hand was decaying.

The tenant escorted the doctor outside. Matýsek went along chiefly to listen whether the coins he had given the doctor and to which Barka had to add a goodly sum, jingled in his pocket as when he himself had owned them. Barka remained in the room alone.

For a while she sat on the bed not knowing what had become of her thoughts, for her head seemed of a sudden, completely empty. She could not even conceive how Matýsek could possibly live without her. Who would tell him on Sundays what he should wear, whether the fur cloak or the top coat? Who would go beside him wearing the green jacket, to church? With whom would he talk, sip, smoke and who in his old age, would stay with him, wait on him, humor him?

She glanced out of the window into the little orchard where Matýsek, leaving to the tenant the further escorting of the doctor, had paused to give another little drill to the children who to-day for the first time had ventured outside.

It was a beautiful evening. On the summits of the snow-covered mountains glowed crowns of roses. The sky resembled a golden sea gradually paling until the first little stars sparkled forth. They smiled at the mountains, rejoicing with them that soon they would be green and glad when the fir groves and the blue violets would pour forth their fragrance, when they would hear the nightingale sing beside the stream, when from every rock a flower would spring and in every furrow the lark would call. Even the stars are sad when they see nothing but snow, frost and ice.

Barka's eyes grew misty and great tears dropped on her clasped hands. For her, spring had come for the last time. But instantly her thoughts returned to Matýsek.

"He need not stay here alone. Now that he has a house, any good and capable woman would marry him. It would be best, perhaps, if I myself would select someone for him. It's a pity, he does not like our tenant. She would never do him any injury."

Just then a young woman, a neighbor, came running into the orchard. She was returning a hatchet which she had borrowed of Matýsek and began joking with him.

"When are you going to get a divorce from your wife so you can marry me?" she laughed. It was the way all the girls talked with him when they met him alone.

Matýsek imagined that each one was in earnest about it. "You'd like to marry me, wouldn't you?" He preened himself, seeming to become a head taller. "I believe it. Others would, too. I have to defend myself against them. But just bear in mind, once for all, that I wouldn't take anyone else than Barka for all of Jerusalem. I wouldn't have left her even if brides owning seven castles had sent word to me from Prague itself."

"And what if you'd become a widower?"

"Get out of here!" Matýsek, red with anger, shouted at the pert young thing, stamping his foot and brandishing the hatchet at her. The girl laughed all the more, but had to run away to escape his wrath.

Barka, lying in tears on the bed, felt as if all the nightingales which were preparing to welcome spring in the mountains had begun to sing in her bosom, all the violets which wished to pour out their fragrance in the groves bloomed in her heart. As Matýsek loved her no other man had ever loved a woman. As happy as they two were, no other husband and wife had ever been, even though one were to seek the whole world over.

She bowed her head meekly and owned that here on this earth she had lived long enough in enjoyment, abundance and happiness and that it was just that her portion should now pass cver to another.

"It would be useless to think of marriage for him. He would have no other, no matter what happened. I must arrange it some other way so that all would go on without me," she said, wiping her eyes. "If only he would not be here when they carry me out. I would have to turn over in my coffin, before they put me in the ground, to know how he would carry on. They say the dead see and hear everything that happens around them before the priest sprinkles their grave. What, dear God, would I see and hear? He will not want to give me up to death and will yet anger God Himself by his stubbornness."

From that time Barka meditated on nothing else than how to contrive to have Matýsek let her go to her grave without too great an ado and too much sorrow and longing for her.

"If I could only last till the time of berries, then I'd take myself off without his knowing," she prayed again and again. So fervently and intensely did she pray for this that, though her hand was now nothing but a mass of wounds and her body only skin and bones, nevertheless she lived through the spring and summer. Everyone who came to see her parted with her forever, for, leaving, they knew they would never again see her alive. Only Matýsek as yet noticed nothing. He had become accustomed to seeing her on the bed all the time and whenever he became thoughtful over her condition, Barka quickly had some joke ready to lead him out of his mood. Well she knew how to turn everything to its cheery phase. It was a trait that stayed with her to her last moment.

On the afternoon just before Holy Mother's Day, before August fifteenth, Matýsek was just finishing a cage for the parish priest, who had ordered it for a rare bird. Matýsek was pleased with it and hopped about it constantly. He was reminded again of his desire to contrive some sort of cage not only for birds, but for the wind also.

This time Barka did not reply as usual that there could be no doubt of it that since people had been able to trap the thunder, he surely could carry out his plan for the wind. He observed her silence and stepped closer to her.

"What is the matter, our Barka, that you talk so little nowadays?" he asked her, patting her bandaged hand and sadly gazing into her sorrowful eyes.

To-day for the first time he noted that she was pale and troubled. She scarcely had any breath left in her. For the first time, perhaps, he had an inkling of what was in store for her.

"It won't last long, this way," Barka consoled him and attempted her customary bright, agreeable smile, which, with effort, she achieved. "This will all change soon. It seems to me I'd get well very quickly if I could only eat some sour berries."

"You can have all you want of those now. In the grove it looks as if the ground had a red coverlet. I saw them when I went there this morning to cut saplings to make bars for the cage."

"Those in our grove wouldn't refresh and strengthen me. If berries are to help me, they must come from Bezděz itself. There every morning the Virgin Mary herself sprinkles them with dew purposely for the sick."

"Someone from here can go up there tomorrow to get them for you."

"I too thought of that. I will ask the tenant to let the children go for them."

"Well, well, they'd be of little use there," burst out Matýsek. "They wouldn't get much and would bring you only brush and bad fruit, ripe, unripe, red, green— all in a bunch. You'd hardly relish that sort of thing. And who knows whether the little imps would ever reach Bezděz. They'd ramble where their fancy suited them and would boldly insist they had actually been there. They'd be of no use except to carry the load. Someone wise and dependable should go with them. Do you know what? I myself shall go with them. No one else can put them through their paces as well as I can."

Barka had him just where she wanted him. He was prepared for a three days' journey, and in the meantime she could set out on hers—to eternity. Already her mild eye was looking into the depths of that eternity, but her lips still smiled. She had sojourned here long enough in happiness, enjoyment and plenty beside her husband who loved her as no man ever loved a woman.

"You're the best man on earth, after all," she whispered to him. "Since we belong to each other, I have never heard a hard word from you. You have never yet done me an injury and you have never once been angry with me. May God bless you for that a hundred thousand times."

Matýsek smiled contentedly, jingling the money in his pocket. "Neither is such a fine disposition as yours possessed by many women on earth. You know how to be cheerful about everything and you can foretell and promise things before they really happen. Only please stop being so thin and pale! And your lips are so blue and how they quiver!"

And again Matýsek patted the bandaged hand and gazed at her with an uncertain, solicitous gaze as before.

I'll be better at once, and as soon as I eat a few of your berries I'll run about like a chick."

"I wish you could do it right now!"

"I shall. I have it all arranged with the Virgin Mary. But when she calls me, I must visit her at Vamberice. She asked it of me last night in a dream and I promised her I'd go."

"You shouldn't have promised her that," complained Matýsek and hung his head. "You gave us your word with uplifted hand that you'd never again go on a pilgrimage."

"This time it will be altogether different," Barka explained. "Our tenant will do everything to suit you much better, and the children, too, are better behaved. Everything will go on as if I were here."

"Oh, no it won't, it won't!" interposed Matýsek and he held on to her feather bed like a child which fears its mother will slip away.

"You'll see that it will," Barka smiled at him but within she felt as if she already stood on God's pillar.

"Just give your orders to the tenant the way you want things done here. She is not a bad woman and will gladly do all to please you and will manage the household well in my absence. She knows that the house and estate will be hers if she serves us both well unto the day of our death, for we have given her our written agreement. Don't stay at home all the time. Go out to different places and visit the neighbors to learn what is happening among people and out in the world and you'll have something to laugh at. Go to church also and say a little prayer for me there. It is good for those who are on a journey if we pray for them at home. I, too, shall always remember you in a prayer. Indeed, I'll do nothing else there than pray for you!"

"Oh, but if you'd only rather stay right here!"

"Keep your things in good order so that they would last. Wear your fur coat whenever you wish, but take care of the top coat, for such a piece of goods you can't again get in a hurry. Those new shirts, the linen for which I spun for you last winter, you know, those with the little red hearts at the collar band, do not wear them all the time. Put them on only on Sundays and holidays so that you'd not wear them out at once, for then you'd have no memento of the work of my hands —and that would grieve me. Don't stop your work. Keep at it every day and in that way you will chase away the loneliness most surely. It will be best if you begin right away to work on that cage in which to shut

up the wind, and when that wearies you, why, just call
the tenant, take a little sip and smoke and have a little
game of cards. . . ."

"Oh, but I'll never drink down the longing for you
nor smoke it away. I know it can't be done," piteously cried poor Matýsek and held on all the more
tightly to Barka's bed covers. Great tears rolled down
his cheeks meanwhile and Barka, unable to gaze longer
at his grief with dry eyes, relieved herself by weeping
with him.

"Do you know what," she sobbed, throwing her well
arm around his neck, "if you will be very lonely and
if you can't get along without me—you need not leave
me there alone. Just start out running after me."

You should have heard into what joyous peals of
laughter Matýsek burst when Barka told him how best
to punish the great loneliness. He was now willing to
let her go on the pilgrimage and no longer offered any
objections, for just as soon as he would be the least bit
lonesome he would start out to meet her there. Barka
would not even be dreaming of it there on her pilgrimage, and suddenly somebody would seize her by the
apron and would refuse to let her go. Yes, she would
see! He'd show her!

If Matýsek had let the children go alone to Bezděz
for the berries, they would have done to a hair exactly
what he prophesied to Barka. His journey passed
quickly, for he often had to stop to scold the children
and give them proper training. Whenever they liked

a spot, they would stop and pick, regardless of where it was. Of little use would they have been to Barka. They had no other thought on the trip than where they could eat the greatest amount of strawberries and blackberries. Their cheeks and hands were constantly painted with them. At every wayside well he had to pause with them and make them wash themselves so that people meeting them would not be too horrified at their appearance. He made up his mind to complain to Barka, that all his trials with them during those three days were unequalled in the history of his troubles and that the berries surely should do her much good.

He drove the children ahead of him like a herd of young goats. Each one bore a load so big that not one person, but ten, could have gotten well from eating the berries. They, too, had a story to tell about that journey to Bezděz for they, likewise, had learned many things they had not before known.

Before the tenant could intercept him he rushed with the children pellmell into the room so that Barka somehow by the very sight of the abundant harvest could have joy. But he paused on the threshold as if he had grown fast to it. The bed beside the window was empty. Barka was nowhere in the room.

It was some time before the tenant could so far control her tears as to follow him. He asked her nothing nor did he even look at her, though he felt her standing beside him.

BARBARA 313

"You're surprised, aren't you, Matýsek?" she finally addressed him, but her thoughts fairly tore her heart.

"You had hardly gone when the mistress became so well suddenly that she got up. She would not let herself be detained, but set out at once on a pilgrimage. She said she had already talked over with you how you'd arrange things here in case you did not find her at home."

Barka had died a few hours after Matýsek's departure. She had felt to a minute the time she was to go and happily she left this world before he returned, just as she had so fervently prayed God might come to pass. She herself had made all arrangements for her funeral, had laid aside the money for it, discussed its details, and prepared for them all. She pleaded with each one in God's name not to divulge to Matýsek that she would never again return home. She hoped that he would gradually get accustomed to the idea of her remaining so long on the pilgrimage.

He,—to get accustomed to being without her!

The tenant softly led Matýsek to the table, though he made no resistance. She brought him something to eat and cared for him just as she had solemnly promised Barka for her own soul's salvation that she would do! Matýsek did not respond to her words. Leaving the food untouched, he sat quietly, motionless, with eyes staring at the bed as if there were not a drop of blood in him.

No coercion could make him go to bed. All night he

sat beside the table looking with vacant gaze at the empty bed.

When the tenant came to him the next day, he was still sitting at the table. It seemed to her he had grown twenty years older and that his hair had suddenly become white. He turned and spoke to her.

"Too much is too much!" he said in a queer hoarse voice. "To go away and stay away,—whoever heard of such a thing? But since she wanted to go, let her stay there. I will do my work here. I'll get along without her."

"You are right," the tenant lauded him. "Let her stay on her pilgrimage if she wants to. We, again, shall stay here. If you are grieved that she left, you'll punish her best by not showing it in the least. Next time, she'll think it over more carefully before she sets out for some place. Just have a little drink and wash down your trouble."

And the tenant brought Matýsek glasses, cards and his pipe just exactly as Barka had ordered her to do. Matýsek quickly seized upon the glass, cards and the pipe with eager hands. But the glass remained full, the pipe went out while he held it in his mouth and of a sudden he did not even know how to name the cards. Alas, he had told her he could not get along without her and yet she had gone and left him. It was no wonder that again he never lay down in bed and remained sitting at the table all night, muttering in a strange voice, "What is too much is too much!"

In his work he fared no better. He set himself to carving, cutting, glueing, but as soon as he tried to put things together nothing seemed to fit. Her merry smile was lacking, her loving words, too, which always made everything clear to him and, when his memory wandered, always led him back to the right path. Now that she was not there to admire and encourage, everything was all confusion to him and no one could seem to straighten things out. Not even a miserable broom was he able to make now, for what he put together in no wise resembled the others.

"What is too much is too much," he whimpered, in his little corner from which he could see so well to the bed. "Until Barka comes back I'll not be able to do a thing worth while, because of grief that she left me in spite of everything."

And idly he remained sitting in his place hour after hour, never taking his eyes from the bed, as if by looking hard he could force her to suddenly appear there at last.

Sometimes he rose and went to the clock to push it ahead so that it would go faster, but after a while he again came back with downcast head. At other times he seized the chalk as if he wished to make marks on the door each day Barka was gone, to count up as he had before, how long before she returned from the pilgrimage. Often he had the door open ready to go to see if she were not already returning, but he never carried out this intention. He pretended to himself that he fully believed in the pilgrimage, but he must have known that she had undertaken a journey from which no one has yet returned, regardless of how much those left longing push the clocks ahead to hasten the moment of reunion or how many chalk marks they make on the door.

Matýsek persuaded himself of his self-deception that Barka had gone to Vamberice only before others. When he stepped before his God he acknowledged the truth. He no longer sat among the married men in the pews at the right, but cowered in the corridor among the beggars who have no one or nothing. There he fell on his knees, pressed the rosary to his lips and those who stood near him heard nothing else during the entire mass except his whispered prayer. "For my dead Barbara, my dead Barbara—"

But when he left the church, he again tried somehow to talk himself out of the fact of her death and whomever he met he asked if they had not met Barka somewhere, and scolded to them that what was too much really was too much, that his wife refused to come back home from the pilgrimage.

And the people did not seek to change him, but assented that it was indeed a burden to have such a roaming wife. Many advised him to leave her where she was and not let her into the house even if she would come back instantly. He nodded in agreement and looked forward to her pleading to be let in. He made up his mind that he would let her beg a long time at the door before he would open it. But—whenever he entered the room where, near the window, stood her vacant bed from which she had smiled at him so earnestly that his work went rapidly and perfectly—like play in fact; from which she had gazed at him so happily that he had been able to do whatever people asked him, he sank again into his chair gazing dully and confusedly into space and his poor mind could not cope with what Fate had sent him.

One morning he arose with brightened brow. It was Sunday and the bells were just ringing for early mass.

"Quickly bring me from the closet the shirt with the red hearts and my blue top-coat also," he ordered the tenant in his accustomed voice and manner.

She was much amazed, for since Barka's death he had never once worn the top-coat. He was taking care of it just as she had instructed him to do and the shirts with the hearts, which had been spun by her own hands, he cherished particularly. Yes, he recalled to a hair every word of hers spoken that evening before she started him on his journey to Bezděz.

"Don't wait for me to-day from church," he said to the tenant.

"And why not?"

"I can't stand it here any longer. I'm going to punish this longing. I shall set out on the road to Vamběřice. Barka told me if I should get lonely while she was gone, that I should start out to meet her, so I'm going. Won't she stare when I suddenly appear before her and say, 'Here I am, our Barka.'"

The tenant thought that he really meant to carry out this oft-repeated threat to lock the door in case Barka should come, and nodding assent to his plans, she gave him his rosary and cane.

Long she looked after him as he walked alone. Tears filled her eyes. She liked to watch Barka and Matýsek walk together to church, for one could tell by the very way they stepped along that they liked to be together here on earth. Poeple laughed, to be sure, and let drop a whisper here and there that they were weak in thoughts, but so few sins as those two had committed surely were to be found in no other household in the entire community.

In vain did the tenant await Matýsek's return to dinner. Her children came running home from church without him all breathless, heated up and frightened. Matýsek, they said, had knelt down in the corridor as usual, and holding his rosary was praying for "dead Barbara," but when, after the mass, all the people stood up, he alone did not arise. When the others had gone out from the church he alone did not leave. They tapped him on the shoulder, but he did not move, only gazed at them strangely. A terror seized the children and they began to scream. The people came running up, picked up Matýsek, tried to bring him back to life, but he remained rigid.

Matýsek had truly gone to find Barka. He could no longer wait. He had punished the longing. And it was no wonder. What is too much, really is too much! . . .

APPENDIX A

THE PRONUNCIATION OF CZECH WORDS

a (unmarked) like u in hut.
o   "   " o " obey.
u   "   " oo " took.
y   "   " y " tryst
á (marked)   " a " palm.
í or ý "   " i " machine.
ú or ů "   " oo " cool.
ě   "   " ye " yet.
aj (semi-diphthong) like y in my.
c (unmarked) like ts in its.
č (marked)   " ch " charm.
ď   "   " d " verdure.
ň   "   " n " canyon.
š   "   " sh " she.
ť   "   " t " future.
ž   "   " z " azure.
ř   "   rolled r plus z as in azure.
j (unmarked) like y in yes.
ch is a guttural as in Scotch "loch."

The suffix -ek gives a diminutive meaning to masculine names, as "Josef," Joseph, but "Josífek," little Joe; Matýs, Matthew, Matýsek, little Matthew. In the same way, -"ka" is a feminine suffix, as in "Barka."

The primary accent always falls on the first syllable in Czech words.

The suffix "-ova" is added to masculine proper names to indicate female members of the family. Thus, Božena Němcová signifies that Božena is of the family or house of Němec.

In "Czech," the English spelling of Čech (Bohemian), the "cz" is pronounced like "ch" in "chair" and the final "ch" like "ch" in the Scotch "loch."

APPENDIX B

THE SLAVS

So many people are under the impression that the Slavic tongues are wholly alien to the other languages of Europe that a brief statement of what groups constitute the Indo-European family of languages will not be amiss. This family includes eight main branches each of which has several sub-divisions. The first or Aryan includes the Indian and the Iranian and those in turn have sub-divisions which are represented by the Sanskrit, the Zend and the old and modern Persian. The second is the Armenian branch. The third is the Hellenic, which includes all the ancient Greek dialects as well as modern Greek. The fourth is the Albanian branch spoken in ancient Illyria and in modern Albania. The fifth is the Italic branch represented by the Latin and other dead dialects and by the modern Romance languages, as French, Italian, Spanish and Portuguese. The sixth is the Celtic branch with sub-divisions of the Gallic, Brittanic and Gaelic and those in their turn represented by the Cornish, Irish, Scotch-Gaelic and Manx. The seventh branch of the Indo-European family is the Teutonic which embraces three main groups, the Gothic, now extinct; the Norse, including the Swedish, Danish, Norwegian and the Icelandic; the West Germanic, which is represented by the German, the Saxon, Flemish, Dutch, Low Franconian, Frisian and English. The eighth branch is the Slavonic, sometimes called Balto-Slavic. The languages developed around the Baltic sea were the old Prussian, the Lithuanian and the Lettic.

A rough division of the Slavs is territorial comprising (I.) Eastern Slavs or Russians, consisting of Great Russians, White Russians and Little Russians, the last named being variously called Ukrainians, Rusins, Ruthenians and Carpatho-Russians. (II.) The Western Slavs, embracing the Czechs (Čechs), Slovaks, Poles, Lusatian Serbs. (III.) The Southern or Jugo-Slavs, including the Slovenes, Serbo-Croats and Bulgarians.

The best authentic division of the Slavs today according to Dr. Lubor Niederle, professor of Archæology and Ethnology at the Czech University at Prague, the capital of Bohemia and also of the new Republic of Czechoslovakia, is as follows:

1. The Russian stem; recently a strong tendency is manifested, toward the recognition within this stem of two nationalities, the Great-Russians and the Small-Russians.

2. The Polish stem; united, with the exception of the small group of the Kašub Slavs, about whom it is as yet uncertain whether they form a part of the Poles or a remnant of the former Baltic Slavs.

3. The Lužice-Serbian stem; dividing into an upper and a lower branch.

4. The Bohemian or Čech and Slovak stem; inseparable in Bohemia and in Moravia, but with a tendency toward individualization among the Slovaks living in what was formerly a part of Hungary.

5. The Slovenian stem.

6. The Srbo-Chorvat (Serbian-Croatian) stem; in which political and cultural, but especially religious,

APPENDIX B

conditions have produced a separation into two nationalities, the Serbian and the Croatian.

7. The Bulgarian stem. Only in Macedonia is it still undecided whether to consider the indigenous Slavs as Bulgarians or Serbians, or perhaps as an independent branch.

The common origin of the Indo-European languages is determined mainly by two tests which the philologists apply. These proofs of kinship are a similar structure or inflectional system and a common root system.

Practically all the common words in use in any of the languages belonging to the Indo-European family are fair illustrations of the strong relationship existing among the eight branches, and are proofs of an original or parent tongue known to nearly all of the now widely dispersed nations of Europe. For instance, the word "mother" in the modern languages has these forms: In the French, it is "mère," abbreviated from the older Italic tongue, Latin, where it was "mater," in the Spanish "madre"; in the German it is "Mutter"; in the Scotch the word becomes "mither"; in the Bohemian or Czech it is "mateř" or "matka"; and in the Russian it is "mat" or "mater."

The English verb, "to be," conjugated in the present tense is:

I am	we are
you are	you are
he is	they are

It is "esse" in the Latin and has, in the present tense, these forms:

sum	sumus
es	estes
est	sunt

In the Czech, the present indicative of "býti" (to be) with the pronouns is:

já jsem	my jsme
ty jsi	vy jste
on jest	oni jsou

The German is:

ich bin	wir sind
du bist	ihr seid
er ist	sie sind

The natural similarity of words in the Slavic languages is obviously even greater and more pronounced than the resemblance of words in the various Indo-European tongues.

Thus, the word "mother" in the principal Slavic tongues has three forms: Russian, mati; Czech, mati; matka or mateř; Serbian, mati; Polish, matka; Bulgarian, majka or mama. The word for "water" is "voda" in all of the above languages except in Polish where it is "woda." The verb "to sit" is, in Russian, sidět; in Czech, seděti; Serbian, sediti; Polish, siedziec; Bulgarian, sědja. One could trace this similarity of roots and suffixes in all the words common in the experience of our ancestors. The examples given are but two of hundreds or even thousands, which conclusively show that the Slavic tongues are philologically related to the other Indo-European tongues.

The etymology of the word "Slav" was not clear for some time. Some philologists connected it with the word "sláva" which means "glory" or "the glorious race." Others, and the numbers of such linguistic students or scholars exceed the former school, have accepted the theory of Joseph Dobrovsky, the Bohemian philologist, who asserted that the term comes from "slovo" which signifies "word" or "those who know words." The term in the original Slavic is "Slovan" which is more closely allied in appearance and sound to the word from which it is derived. Dobrovsky claimed that the earliest ancestors of the present Slavs called themselves "Slované" or "men who knew words or languages" in contradistinction to the Germans who did not know their words or language and hence were called "Němci" from "Němý" meaning "dumb." The Slavic name for Germans, oddly enough, has remained "Němci" or "the dumb ones" to this day. This dubbing of a neighbor nation which is dissimilar in language and customs recalls the practice of the ancient Greeks who named all other nations who were not Greeks "barbarians."

The name "Czech" or "Čech" as it is correctly written, should by all rights be the only title applied to the group of Slavic people occupying the 22,000 square miles in what was Northern Austria. It is a word originally designating the leader of the small band of Slavs who, in the fifth century, emigrating from Western Russia, settled in the valley of the Vltava (Moldau) in the heart of Europe and there have remained as the sturdy vanguard of the Slav people. General Fadejév well said in 1869 "Without Bohemia the Slav cause is forever lost; it is the head, the advance guard, of all Slavs." From the word "Čech" is derived the poetic name "Čechia" for Bohemia, this term corresponding to our symbolic "Columbia" for America.

The names "Bohemia" and "Bohemians" as applied to the country and to this group of Slavs respectively, are derived from the word "Boji," or "Boii," a Celtic tribe, occupying the basin of the Vltava and the Elbe before the permanent settlement there of the Czechs. Julius Cæsar in his "Commentaries on the Gallic Wars" speaks frequently of the "Boji" and "Marcomanni." The word "Boii" was in the Latinized form, "Bojohemum," applied to the country of those early Celts who had occupied the country and eventually the name "Bojohemum" was changed to "Bohemia." In the later days, the Slav inhabitants became known as "Bohemians" to the outside races unfamiliar with the correct term "Čech" which to facilitate pronunciation by non-Slavs is written "Czech." The "Cz" is pronounced like "Ch" in "child," the "e" like in "net," and the final "ch" is pronounced like "h" sounded gutturally.

When the Magyars or Hungarians, a Mongolian tribe, invaded Hungary, they spelled disaster to Slavic unity for, linguistically and racially, they were so different from the Czechs and Slovaks that they have ever been a scourge and a menace to those two Slavic peoples.

The Slovaks, most nearly allied in language and customs to the Czechs, occupy the fields and Carpathian mountains of northern Hungary. A splendid and ancient history is theirs though in latter centuries it has become one continuous record of bitter oppression suffered first at the hands of the Tatar invaders and then from the cruel Magyars of Hungary and of the always privileged Germans of the Hapsburg domain. Slovakia suffered the misfortune of being incorporated with Hungary in the tenth century and Magyarization has gone on relentlessly as a result. The Slovak language has been wonderfully developed since the time of Anton Bernolák but every means, every fiendish device has been used by the Magyars to utterly exterminate the

APPENDIX B

race speaking it and to crush out completely all memory of the tongue hated so desperately by the Hungarians. It must not be forgotten that the Hungarian Count Tisza now of tainted fame and unmourned memory, on December 15, 1875, said on the floor of the Hungarian Parliament, "There is no Slovak nation." He had done his best to annihilate it but it has lived just as the spirit of France has lived in Alsace-Lorraine despite the superhuman efforts of Hungary's ally to Germanize the "Lost Provinces." Over 2,000,000 Slovaks live in Hungary and nearly a million have emigrated to this country as much to avoid the persecutions of the Magyars as to earn the advantages of America.

APPENDIX C

BIBLIOGRAPHY OF CZECH AND SLOVAK LITERATURE

Bačkovský, Dr. F. Přehled Písemnictví Českého. Dr. Ed. Grégr. Prague. 1899.

Bowring, Sir John. (Wýbor z básnictví českého.) Cheskian Anthology. Being a history of the Poetical Literature of Bohemia, with translated specimen. 270 pp. Howland Hunter. St. Paul's Church Yard. London. 1832.

Flajšhans, Dr. V. Nejstarší Památky Jazyka i Písemnictví Českého. Fr. Bačkovský. Prague. 1903.

Hrbek, Jeffrey D. List of books in English relating to Bohemians and Bohemia. Osvěta Americká. Omaha. 1908.

Jesenský, Dr. Jan. Nástin Dějin Slovenskej Literatury. Československá Tlačova Kancelár. Ekaterinburg, Siberia. 1918.

Jireček, Josef. Rukovětí k Dějinám Literatury České do Konce XVIII. Věku. Časopis Českého Musea. Prague. 1875–1876.

Jungmann, Josef. Historie Literatury České. V. Tomek. Prague. 1849.

Lutzow, Count. Lectures on the Historians of Bohemia; being the Ilchester Lectures for the year 1904. 120 pp. Henry Frowde. London. 1905.

Lutzow, Count. A History of Bohemian Literature. 425 pp. D. Appleton and Company. New York. 1899.

Morfill, Richard William. The Dawn of European

Literature. Slavonic Literature. 264 pp. Society for Promoting Christian Knowledge. London. 1888.

Ninger, Karel. Historie Literatury České. I. L. Kober. Prague. 1874.

Novák, Dr. Jan V. Dr. Arne Novák. Přehledné Dějiny Literatury České. R. Prombergr. Olomouc. 1913.

Ottův Naučný Slovnik (Otto Encyclopedia). Articles on Czech, Slovak and western Slav literature, by Fr. Bilý, Jos. Hanuš, F. X. Šalda, Ant. Truhlář, Jan Vobornik, Jaroslav Vrchlický.

Pypin, A. N. and V. D. Spasovič. Přel. Antonín Kotík. Historie Literatur Slovanských. Fr. Šimaček. Prague. 1882.

Selver, P. An Anthology of Modern Bohemian Poetry. 128 pp. Henry J. Drane. London. 1912.

Tieftrunk, Karel. Historie Literatury České. Edw. Grégr. Prague. 1885.

Vlček, Jaroslav. Literatura Česká Devatenáctého Století. Jan Laichter. Prague. 1902–1907. Čestí Spisovatelé XIX Století. Prague. 1904. Dějiny Literatury Slovenskej. Prague. 1890.

Wratislaw, A. H. The Native Literature of Bohemia in the Fourteenth Century. Four lectures delivered before the University of Oxford on the Ilchester Foundation. 174 pp. Geo. Bell and Sons. London. 1878.

THE END